THE
NEW TEACHER
TOOLBOX

SECOND EDITION

PROVEN TIPS AND STRATEGIES
FOR **A GREAT FIRST YEAR**

D1303803

SCOTT M.
MANDEL

CORWIN
A SAGE Company

For information:

Corwin
A SAGE Company
2455 Teller Road
Thousand Oaks, California 91320
(800) 233-9936
Fax: (800) 417-2466
www.corwinpress.com

SAGE India Pvt. Ltd.
B 1/I 1 Mohan Cooperative Industrial Area
Mathura Road, New Delhi 110 044
India

SAGE Ltd.
1 Oliver's Yard
55 City Road
London EC1Y 1SP
United Kingdom

SAGE Asia-Pacific Pte. Ltd.
33 Pekin Street #02-01
Far East Square
Singapore 048763

Printed in the United States of America.

Library of Congress Cataloging-in-Publication Data

Mandel, Scott M.
The new teacher toolbox : proven tips and strategies for a great first year / Scott M. Mandel. — 2nd ed.
   p. cm.
Includes bibliographical references and index.
ISBN 978-1-4129-7134-8 (cloth)
ISBN 978-1-4129-7135-5 (pbk.)
  1. First year teachers. 2. Teachers—In-service training. I. Title.

LB2844.1.N4M26 2009
371.1—dc22   2008051640

This book is printed on acid-free paper.

09 10 11 12 13 10 9 8 7 6 5 4 3 2 1

Acquisitions Editor:	Carol Chambers Collins
Editorial Assistant:	Brett Ory
Production Editor:	Jane Haenel
Copy Editor:	Claire Larson
Typesetter:	C&M Digitals (P) Ltd.
Proofreader:	Sue Irwin
Indexer:	Sheila Bodell
Cover and Graphic Designer:	Scott Van Atta

Contents

Acknowledgments   v

About the Author   vi

Introduction: What New Teachers Really Want to Know   1

Part I: The Room Environment and the First Weeks   5

1. Things to Do Before the School Year Begins   6
2. Arranging Your Classroom   15
3. Bulletin Boards   18
4. A Helpful Binder to Leave for Substitute Teachers   22

Part II: The Curriculum and the Students   25

5. Fairness and Critical Thinking in Classroom Discussions   26
6. Teaching Five Hours of Material in Only Three Hours   32
7. Keeping Students Interested   37
8. Teaching Test-Taking Skills   42
9. The Internet as the Ultimate Teacher Resource Center   46
10. Discipline Issues   50

Part III: Grading   56

11. Marking Papers and Promoting Self-Esteem   57
12. A Beginner's Guide to Figuring Grades   60
13. Rubrics   66
14. Grading for Classroom Participation   71
15. A Student Self-Esteem Check   74

Part IV: Parents   79

16. Parent Involvement   80
17. Parent-Teacher Conferences   86

Part V: Students Who Have Special Needs   **90**

18. Modifying the Classroom Curriculum
    for Students With Special Needs   91
19. Full-Inclusion Mainstreaming   95
20. Students With ADD/ADHD and Classroom Management   98
21. Preparing for a Special Education Class   102

Part VI: How to Maintain Your Sanity   **106**

22. Making It Through Your Teacher Evaluation   107
23. Ten Ways to Avoid Stress   112
24. Putting It All Into Perspective   116

Further Reading   **122**

References   **125**

Index   **126**

Acknowledgments

Many hands went into the production of this book. First of all, I want to thank the wonderful people at Corwin. Working with them on this book has been a writer's pleasure! I want to thank my editor, Carol Collins, for her brilliant job with my words. I also want to thank Scott Van Atta for his wonderful design work on the cover.

A number of excellent educators in the Los Angeles Unified School District lent their invaluable feedback, ideas, and suggestions to these pages. These people reviewed the material from a variety of different perspectives in the attempt to make the book as valuable as possible to new teachers: mentor teachers Melodie Bitter, Jo Schillinger, and Robert Schuck; school administrators in charge of new-teacher education Robert Krell and Aaron Moretzsky; local district coordinator, instructional support services, Ann Carnes; and most important, new classroom teachers Jennifer Bankston and Jennifer Hitchcock. Editorial assistance on the second edition was provided by Kathie Marshall, Robert Schuck, Robert Krell, and Melodie Bitter.

A number of excellent lessons originally submitted to the Web site Teachers Helping Teachers (www.pacificnet.net/~mandel) were so good that I adapted their ideas to these pages. I thank Diane Clark, Jan Demontigny, Daniel Duffy, Debora Mcdonnell, Tony Murphy, Jean Roberts, and Teresa Wasinger for their wonderful ideas.

PUBLISHER'S ACKNOWLEDGMENT

Corwin gratefully acknowledges the contributions of the following reviewer:

Toni Jones
Principal, Elementary Education
Bonita, CA

About the Author

In his more than 25 years as an educator, **Scott M. Mandel** has served as a teacher, an administrator, and an inservice leader. Currently, he teaches English and history at the Pacoima Middle School Television, Theatre, and Performing Arts Magnet in Los Angeles. He received his Ph.D. in curriculum and instruction from the University of Southern California; his current areas of professional specialization include new-teacher training, improving test-taking and study skills, classroom management, teaching methodologies, the parent-teacher partnership, and using the Internet in educational settings. A National Board Certified teacher, Scott is the author of ten previous books as well as the founder and developer of Teachers Helping Teachers (www.pacificnet.net/~mandel), a Web site for educators. Teachers Helping Teachers has been offering lesson plans, educational links, and inspiration since 1995.

This book is dedicated to the most important person in my life, Melodie Bitter.
For over twenty years, Melodie has been my best friend, proofreader of my books,
associate director of my student shows, and partner in just about everything professional
I have experienced. She's also, without question, the best teacher I have ever met.
It is fitting that this book on teaching be dedicated to her.

Introduction

What New Teachers Really Want to Know

Aliya was an energized first-year teacher. Teaching had been her dream, her calling, her goal ever since she was a little girl. She graduated from a top teacher education program and was hired after her second interview. She was ready for and excited about her first year of teaching.

But the reality of the classroom was quite different from what she expected.

The large city district in which she was employed provided monthly new-teacher workshops. She enthusiastically attended the August meeting, two weeks before school began. There they taught her all about the state standards.

What Aliya really wanted to know was, "What do I need to do my first week of class?"

The district response was either to ask someone at her school, or to use her mentor teacher (who would not be assigned until the third week of school). After all, she was informed, new-teacher meetings were for the "important material," and nothing was more important for a new teacher than knowing the state standards.

Aliya disagreed but remained quiet, not wanting to get into trouble. She stumbled through her first month in the classroom.

Frustrated, and a little scared, Aliya looked forward to the new-teacher workshop for the month of September. At that meeting, the subject was "Creating Rubrics to Match the State Standards."

What Aliya really wanted to know was how to conduct her first parent-teacher conference, scheduled in two weeks.

In response to her questions, she was directed to concentrate on the material at hand.

Aliya disagreed but remained quiet, not wanting to get into trouble. Consequently, she felt her first parent-teacher conference was a fiasco, and she left in tears.

Frustrated, scared, and unsure of her abilities, Aliya went to the new-teacher workshop in October. She was concerned because it was taking her hours to prepare her first report cards. In addition, she was dissatisfied with those she had finished. She was still looking for answers. But the workshop's topic was "How to Begin Preparing for the Spring Standardized Exams."

Aliya disagreed, but this time, she decided to keep her mouth shut.

Aliya skipped the November new-teacher workshop.

New teachers often exit their university education programs and enter their own classrooms having been taught "everything they need to know." Through their coursework and in-class experiences, they have learned how to teach a poem, introduce long division, or set up a science experiment. Teachers employed based on an emergency teaching license may not even have that information.

Districts often provide additional inservice help in areas such as how to

- align the curriculum to the state standards,
- teach to the state standards, and
- prepare students for the state standardized tests.

As our new teacher, Aliya, discovered on her own, these topics do not address the classroom reality.

A REALITY CHECK

During my tenure as a mentor teacher, I have rarely been asked questions about teaching methodologies or about teaching to the standards. Rather, I most often hear the following questions:

- What do I need to do to prepare for the first day?
- Why can't I get my students to behave in class?
- What's the best way to arrange my classroom?
- Why does it take me so long to prepare my grades?
- What can I do about parents who are upset about their child's grade?
- How can I alleviate the stress?

Many education classes and district new-teacher programs address the following topics, but unfortunately on a limited basis:

- Daily classroom management techniques
- Developing a fair and easily organized grading system
- Working with parents
- Keeping your sanity

THE PURPOSE OF THIS BOOK

This book is designed to provide you with practical solutions and ideas in the areas listed previously. Written by an everyday classroom teacher, in consultation with other mentor teachers, this information is concise and easily adapted to most classrooms. You do not need to read the full text to locate relevant information; nor do you need to buy into a particular educational philosophy. This book is eclectic, practical, and adaptable. Some of the ideas in these pages will directly relate to your teaching situation; some will not. Choose only the advice that specifically interests you and is helpful to your particular situation.

HOW TO USE THIS BOOK

Each part is divided into chapters with easy-to-follow subsections:

- A real-life anecdote, introducing the problem
- The basic issue the chapter addresses
- The grade levels to which the chapter's issue is most applicable (not every issue is relevant to every grade)
- A timeline for when you should focus on this issue during the school year
- The idea for addressing the issue (note: this section is not titled "Solutions," for there are no absolute solutions; all ideas need to be adapted to your particular situation and your individual teaching style)
- Concluding thoughts: a summary of the major points presented
- A few recent, excellent resources for further reading on this subject, if you want to go into greater depth in this particular subject

WHAT'S NEW IN THIS EDITION

In the six years since the first edition of *The New Teacher Toolbox*, I have received hundreds of comments and suggestions on how to make this book even better. The following are areas new to this edition:

- *Updated Information for Today's Classroom in the Age of No Child Left Behind (NCLB).* When this book was originally written, NCLB was relatively new. Since then, virtually every classroom in the country has been affected by its requirements and consequences. Material throughout the book has been updated to reflect this new reality, and what it means for the new teacher.
- *New Ideas and a New Chapter.* I have included many of the wonderful ideas offered over the past six years, adding to what was already here, and substituting better ones when appropriate. For example, the new chapter, "Making It Through Your Teacher Evaluation" (Chapter 22), is a direct result of new teacher feedback on the first edition.
- *Updated Internet Sites and Resources.* A lot has changed in six years—links have been updated or replaced, and new resources added.

- *More Resources for In-Depth Study.* It is impossible for this introductory book to go into great detail for every subject presented. However, there are some areas where you may want additional information or alternative ideas. This section will supply a couple of additional resources for those teachers who want to go into greater depth in a particular subject.

As you read this book, remember that every teacher is different; every teacher is unique. The ideas presented in this second edition must be stylized, adapted, and molded into what works for *you*. The ideas are generalized, with emphasis on the underlying transferable philosophies. As a result, this book will fit every teacher's individual situation.

Above all, you need to make the material in this book work for your individual teaching environment. It's your classroom and your life for almost seven hours, five days a week.

PART I

The Room Environment and the First Weeks

✓ **Things to Do Before the School Year Begins**

What do I need to do before the first day of school?

✓ **Arranging Your Classroom**

How can I organize the physical classroom to create the most efficient learning environment?

✓ **Bulletin Boards**

What types of material should I include on my bulletin boards?

✓ **A Helpful Binder to Leave for Substitute Teachers**

What can I do to prepare a substitute teacher for taking over my classroom?

1

Things to Do Before the School Year Begins

The opening staff meeting had just ended, and Aliya walked into her classroom. It was bare. There were no supplies. She didn't know what she needed to do first, or second, or third. She knew she needed pencils and paper and basic supplies. She knew she needed to create bulletin boards. However, what she really needed was direction.*

Grade Levels

K–12

Timeline

From two weeks before school begins through the first week of school

The Issue

What do I need to do before the first day of school?

---

*Basic ideas in this chapter contributed by Teresa Wasinger, Pleasant Valley Middle School, Wichita, Kansas.

THE IDEA

To prepare your classroom effectively, you must complete a number of tasks, procure a number of items, and make a number of decisions. The following to-do list includes the most important areas to address early on:

- Arrange the classroom.
- Get supplies.
- Gather basic information about the school.
- Prepare for the first day.
- Organize the first week's curriculum.
- Establish procedures.

ARRANGE THE CLASSROOM

When planning the physical layout of your classroom, consider the following ideas:

- Decide on a classroom theme: Choose a major subject area your students will study during the first month of school, such as one of the following examples:
  - ✓ Number sense
  - ✓ Poetry
  - ✓ The Civil War
  - ✓ The solar system

  Keep your theme in mind as you arrange the room, particularly when creating bulletin board notices, a welcome sign, and any other decorative room materials.
- Gather bulletin board materials and create bulletin boards (see Chapter 3 on how to create effective bulletin boards).
  - ✓ Ask an experienced teacher on staff, the school office manager, or secretary what bulletin board materials are available, where they are kept, and how they can be procured.
  - ✓ Visit a local teacher-resource store—it will become your home away from home your first year. You can locate over a thousand high-quality teacher stores using the Web site of the NSSEA—National School Supply and Equipment Association (www.teacherstores.com). (Save the receipts. They may be tax-deductible.)
- Decide where to post notices. Choose a prominent, easily accessible place where all students can check every day for pertinent information, such as near or on the door or at the front of the room.
- Make a classroom welcome sign.
- Arrange desks, learning centers, display tables, and student work areas. Choose an arrangement that enables you to have the most student contact within the physical restrictions of the room (see Chapter 2, "Arranging Your Classroom," for more details).

Teacher Tool

Be sure to have on hand the following indispensable bulletin board items:

- Construction paper
- Push pins or a stapler and staples
- Border (available at educational supply stores or make your own)

Collect the following items throughout the year:

- Curricular materials, including pictures and artifacts, pertaining to themes you will teach—the Internet is a terrific resource for these materials (see Chapter 9, "The Internet as the Ultimate Teacher Resource Center")
- Generic sayings, slogans, and information you can use anytime throughout the year (such as "Never settle for less than your best")

GET SUPPLIES

Some supplies will be given to you; some you will have to request. There are many things you will not realize you need until you need them. The following is a list of those supplies virtually every teacher needs at some point during the school year. Most of these will be available at your school. For those you purchase, be sure to save the receipts. You may be reimbursed later in the year; if not, they may be tax-deductible. Parents can donate some of the items (for example, have each child bring in one box of tissues). You might even send home a list of needed supplies, asking parents to donate anything they can.

Table 1.1   Student and Teacher Supplies

Student Work Supplies	Teacher Supplies
• Writing, drawing, and construction paper • Pencils and pens • Crayons • Paste or glue	• Stapler and staples • Paper clips • Rubber bands • Transparent tape • Manila folders • Marking pens (green or blue, not red; see the section in Part III on marking papers and promoting self-esteem) • Rulers • Art supplies (appropriate for projects you have in mind for the school year—get these now before your school possibly runs out) • Grade and roll book

Items Students Request	Teacher Supplies
• Straight and safety pins • Adhesive bandages • Tissues	• Lesson plan book • Attendance materials (check with your school administrator in charge of attendance) • Textbooks and workbooks • Boxes for storage and portfolios • USB flash drive for transferring files and information between your home and school computers

GATHER BASIC INFORMATION ABOUT THE SCHOOL

Every school has its own procedures. Some are explicitly told to you, some are in the faculty handbook (if provided), and some you are expected to learn on your own. In addition, every school is its own community. You need to learn whom you can approach for help and whom to avoid because they have their own agendas. Learning about school procedures and people will assist you in becoming a successful member of the school community.

Your first step is to discover who has the information about school procedures and resources. Your administrator or fellow teachers should be able to provide most of the information you need (see Chapter 23, "Ten Ways to Avoid Stress," for more tips on seeking advice from fellow teachers). The keeper of the majority of school information, however, is the office manager or school secretary (who may also be able to put you in touch with other teachers before the school year begins). This person is critical for you to befriend and go to for assistance.

Following is a list of the minimum information you need to find out about your school:

- Emergency drills (that is, fire, earthquake, tornado, lock-down)
  - ✓ Where does your class assemble?
  - ✓ What ancillary duties may be assigned?
- Bell schedule
  - ✓ What is the time period for each class and break?
  - ✓ Are there special bell schedules for certain days?
- Lunch and recess procedures
  - ✓ Are you assigned to supervise, and if so, when, how, and where?
  - ✓ Do you need to escort your students or meet them at a special location or time?
- Pullout sessions
  - ✓ Do you need to plan for students leaving your class at regular times for such things as orchestra, chorus, special education services, or gifted activities?

- Staff handbook
  - ✓ Is there a resource to answer your questions, a written document containing at minimum the necessary information on procedures?
- Your colleagues
  - ✓ Who is the administrator responsible for your subject area or grade level and your evaluation?
  - ✓ Whom can you turn to for help?
  - ✓ Who is your grade-level or department chair?
  - ✓ Who is your union representative?

Learning about school procedures and people will assist you in becoming a successful member of the school community.

- Discipline
  - ✓ What are your school's disciplinary procedures?
  - ✓ How does your school handle referrals?

- Support staff
  - ✓ Which nonclassroom personnel do you see for personnel questions? Student information? Supply questions?
  - ✓ Who cleans your room?
  - ✓ Who is responsible for facility maintenance?
  - ✓ What can you do to help them (such as having students put chairs up on the desks)?

Teacher Tool

Never inform students that this is your first teaching assignment.

PREPARE FOR THE FIRST DAY

When the students come into class the first day, you set the tone for the entire year—you are making a first impression. The more organized you are, the stronger the positive image you project. This is especially important in the secondary grades. (If you will be teaching a special education class, see Part V, "Students Who Have Special Needs," for additional advice on handling the first day.)

The following ideas will help you prepare for a successful first day:

- Create nametags for students.
  - ✓ Elementary and first-year middle school students feel more welcomed if you have nametags prepared for them. An alternative is having a nameplate for each student's desk (made by folding cardboard in half or into a prism shape).
- Prepare a packet of first-day materials to send home:
  - ✓ Emergency cards
  - ✓ School rules

    ✓ Bus regulations and information
    ✓ Welcome letter to parents
    ✓ Your classroom expectations and schedule

- Prepare a class list. Note any important information that you may need to locate or check on, such as an address or telephone number.
- Decide on a seating plan. Assigning students in alphabetical order often helps in learning their names.
- Review student records to locate any with special needs, such as gifted, special education, and non-English-speaking students. Identify these students in your roll book.
- Review all individualized education plans (IEPs) and individual accommodation plans under Section 504 (504s) and note your responsibilities. If these are not readily available, see the administrator in charge of these special needs programs. Often the records have not been received from the previous school (particularly in the case of first-year middle school and high school students). If for any reason they are not accessible to you, ask when they will be and note the date. Be sure to follow up. You can also seek out last year's teachers to talk to them regarding accommodations for IEP, 504, or students with special needs (your official classroom roster should designate students in these categories). This will help you be prepared for possible problems from the first day.
- Every day (but especially on the first day) write the daily schedule, date, your name, and classroom goals for the day on the board. Do this before students enter so they see the information as they walk in. It immediately adds to their comfort level. Many teachers also provide their students with their e-mail address (but not their phone numbers).
- Think of a signal for gaining student attention that you will use from the first day. This *must* be grade appropriate. Typical signals are raising your hand, three claps, ringing a bell, and turning out the lights. Talk to others in your grade level for appropriate ways to signal your students.

Teacher Tool

Ask your peers for advice about what to include in your first-day materials, including how to find out such information as bus regulations and school rules. Many teachers will share what they have used, and some schools have grade-level handouts. Ask to see some "welcome" letters they have used, which you could adapt.

ORGANIZE THE FIRST WEEK'S CURRICULUM

As you are getting ready for the first day, you should also start to plan for the entire week. That first week is hectic—the more you do before the year begins, the better you will feel come that first weekend.

- Brainstorm class expectations. Begin accumulating ideas about where you want to take the students over the first few weeks, in terms of both the curriculum and class work habits and norms.
- Create lesson plans for the first week. Be prepared to be flexible as you adapt to your students' personalities and work styles and deal with unexpected school interruptions, textbooks not distributed until later in the month, and potential class and schedule changes. (See Chapter 18, "Modifying the Classroom Curriculum for Students with Special Needs," for additional information on modifying your lesson plan for students with special needs.)

Teacher Tool

Many of your colleagues can share first-week introductory lessons. You can also find a number of first-week lessons for all subjects and grades every August and September on the Teachers Helping Teachers Web site: www.pacificnet.net/~mandel.

- Duplicate materials for the first week. Be prepared. Over-prepare.
- Create some sponge activities for students to do in case of first-week interruptions. *Sponge activities* are short activities that the students can do on their own for five to fifteen minutes, such as "Create a list of things with four legs."
  - ✓ See the Web site www.innovativeclassroom.com/Teaching_Toolbox/#Sponge Activities for sponge activity ideas.
- Prepare files for parent correspondence, school bulletins, and substitute teachers.

You will need these files sooner than you expect to, so prepare them as soon as possible. (See the Chapter 4, "A Helpful Binder to Leave for Substitute Teachers," for details.) Include in these files various standard forms that you will need throughout the year, such as field trip permission forms.

ESTABLISH PROCEDURES

Every school culture is different; every classroom culture is different. What's normal in one school or one class may not be normal for another. Sometimes you have complete freedom to do what you want to do; sometimes entire grade levels or departments have general procedures that you are expected to follow. Ask your administrator or department chair if there are established procedures, or if you have the freedom to select your own.

The following areas are normally determined by the school, grade level, or department:

- Book distribution procedures
- Homework schedules, including days for subject assignments when there is departmentalization of homework
- Acceptable formats and procedures for written assignments (this is especially applicable to many English departments and where there is interdisciplinary team teaching)
- Classroom or school computer use

The following areas are normally determined by the classroom teacher:

- Procedures for turning in work
- Format of work (when not established by the department)
- Procedures for handing back assignments to students
- Homework standards
- Grading standards and procedures for recording grades
- Extra-credit assignments and portfolios
- Housekeeping procedures, such as cleaning up and storing supplies
- Rewards and incentives
- Communication with parents (although record keeping for this is often school-determined)
- Daily routines, including opening procedures, transition times, and independent and group work times and procedures

> What's normal in one school or one class may not be normal for another.

- Daily agenda use (such as meeting agendas)
- Motivators

Class Rules

Your rules chart creates for the students the atmosphere of the classroom; unfortunately, these charts are typically composed of negative rules. These set a tone for the student, and a preconception of what your classroom may be like. The following are actual examples, including the potential student reaction:

- No hitting, pushing, fighting, or running. (The teacher thinks that we're going to act up, so we have to be told what is not acceptable before it even occurs.)
- Sit silently in your seat and raise your hand. (The teacher is the dictator, and we are being treated like little kids.)

Negative classroom rules create negative attitudes. If you need to post rules, make them positive rules that acknowledge the students' common sense. This is especially true in Grade 4 and higher, when the students have been in school a number of years and know from experience what is expected and acceptable. You might even ask for student input when creating rules. Examples of positive rules include the following:

(Continued)

(Continued)

- Respect everyone in the room.
- Respect everything in the room.
- Respect the words (for a language arts class), numbers (for a math class), life (for a biology class), music, or art.

Subsequent classroom discussions can go into what respect means, based on that particular class, with those individual students, at that specific age. In this fashion, you can discuss all of the negative rules without having them posted in front of students' faces all year.

CONCLUDING THOUGHTS

Be prepared. You need to anticipate, prepare, and plan for what you will need throughout the year. This includes arranging the room environment, getting supplies, discovering what information is important to know about the school and your class, preparing for the first day, organizing the first week's curriculum, understanding various school and department procedures, and establishing your own procedures and class rules.

FOR FURTHER READING ON THIS SUBJECT

Corcoran, J. (2007). *First year teacher: Wisdom, warnings, and what I wish I'd known my first 100 days on the job.* New York: Kaplan Publishing.

Glasgow, N. A., & Hicks, C. D. (2009). *What successful teachers do: 101 research-based classroom strategies for new and veteran teachers* (2nd ed.). Thousand Oaks, CA: Corwin.

Moran, C., Stobbe, J. C., Baron, W., Miller, J., & Moir, E. (2008). *Keys to the elementary classroom: A new teacher's guide to the first month of school* (3rd ed.). Thousand Oaks, CA: Corwin.

2

Arranging Your Classroom

Aliya needed to arrange her room. She was supplied with rectangular student tables, where two students could easily sit at every table. She knew that the traditional setup was to make rows of student seats; however, she didn't want to do that. In her university work, she had learned that the farther a student sits from the teacher, the more apt he or she is to be off-task. How could Aliya set up her classroom to maximize teacher-student interaction?

Grade Levels

2–12

Timeline

Two or three days before school begins

The Issue

How can I organize the physical classroom to create the most efficient learning environment?

THE IDEA

Student seats in classrooms are traditionally set in rows or in clusters of three or four tables (for cooperative learning); however, there are fundamental problems with each of these arrangements.

Studies have shown that the farther back a student sits in the room, the higher the number of discipline problems that student will have (see, for example, Paine, 1983; and Daly & Suite, 1981). When the teacher is centered in, and limited to, the front of the classroom, visual, aural, and physical stimulation increasingly diminishes the farther the students sit from the teacher. Consequently, boredom occurs, potentially leading to disruptive behavior.

When students are arranged in groups of four or six, the opposite is often true. Students become overstimulated by their peers in the group. There are now *more* distractions, making it harder for the teacher to keep the students focused on any instruction.

A workable alternative is to arrange the chairs and tables into a U-shape (with an occasional second row on the inside if class size and room demand). See the diagrams in Figure 2.1.

In this arrangement, the teacher not only teaches in the front of the class but also within the large open middle section, and *every student is in the first or second row*. The teacher can move freely around the room while talking, therefore providing continual personal contact with each student.

The result of this arrangement is significant. Student attention is greater and fewer discipline problems occur. In addition, you will find that it is quite adaptable. The students can easily move desks or tables around within two to three minutes when you wish to use cooperative learning groups.

Figure 2.1   The Physical Arrangement of the Student Desks

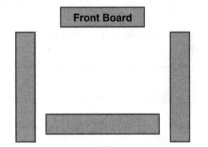

Single row: Good for classes of 15–24 students

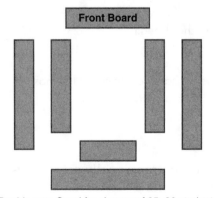

Double row: Good for classes of 25–32 students

Desk arrangement isn't the only consideration when preparing your room. You should add special features that make it a pleasant place for the students. Doing this will affect their mood upon entering the class. For example, include plants, posters, and a comfortable reading corner (especially in the elementary grades). Depending on the physical components of the room, you may need to think about where the students will put their textbooks, coats, and backpacks. If places for these items are not readily available, a personal investment in plastic crates may be the answer. Keeping the clutter to a minimum and having a place for everything is essential. (See also Chapter 21, "Preparing for a Special Education Class," for additional specific ideas for adapting your classroom.)

CONCLUDING THOUGHTS

Arrange the student desks to maximize teacher-student interaction, while remaining flexible for cooperative learning groups. Whenever possible, be sure that no student is farther than two rows away from you. Also plan for a pleasant environment, one that sets the mood and reduces everyday clutter in the classroom.

FOR FURTHER READING ON THIS SUBJECT

Bothmer, S. (2003). *Creating the peaceable classroom: Techniques to calm, uplift, and focus teachers and students*. Tucson, AZ: Zephyr Press.
Google.com. Use search term "Classroom Arrangement" for articles and examples online.
Heiss, R. (2004). *Feng shui for the classroom: 101 easy-to-use ideas*. Chicago: Zephyr Press.

3

Bulletin Boards

One of the first tasks that Aliya focused on after arranging her students' seats was to decide what to include on her bulletin boards. She remembered that most bulletin boards from her student-teaching experiences were either full of the students' work or based on a holiday. Obviously, she had no work to post, and her students were a little too old to be impressed with holiday boards. She wasn't sure what to do.

Grade Levels

K–12

Timeline

All year, but especially the week before school begins

The Issue

What types of material should I include on my bulletin boards?

THE IDEA

Bulletin boards are too often used only for displaying student work. If you look at your classroom environment holistically, however, you will note that bulletin boards can be a major component of the classroom curriculum. You can use them to provide important classroom information or curricular material, or just to stimulate your students to think a little more every time they look at the boards.

Bulletin board material should not be limited to the board itself. You can, and should, use all blank walls. This is especially true in new classroom bungalows, where an entire wall is made of a fabric-like material, allowing the use of pins to display material. In the following discussion, *bulletin boards* refer to all walls with potential for displaying material.

There are four distinct types of bulletin boards that should be used in every classroom at least one time during the year:

- Informational boards
- Philosophical boards
- Curricular boards
- Show-off boards

(See Chapter 16, "Parent Involvement," for discussion of another type of board that showcases particular students' families and cultures.)

INFORMATIONAL BOARDS

Informational boards are those devoted to school schedules, school and classroom procedures, and the dreaded class rules (see Chapter 1, "Things to Do Before the School Year Begins," for more information about creating class rules). The content of these boards is straightforward, but remember that the tone of even straightforward information, such as class rules, can influence student attitudes.

PHILOSOPHICAL BOARDS

This type of bulletin board usually contains commercially produced posters with sayings that make the students feel good. The sayings should remind the students to think, but avoid those that are overly corny, especially if the students are older.

Posters with special messages are often effective. One of my favorites is a colorful poster called "How to Be An Artist," by SARK. It contains short phrases such as "splash through puddles" and "take naps." Another good one is "All I Ever Really Needed to Know I Learned in Kindergarten," by Robert Fulghum. These types of posters initiate student thinking and leave them with a good feeling without talking down to them.

You can find these posters at your local teacher store. You can also locate a lot of free educational materials online at www.freebies.about.com/od/teacherfreebies/Teacher_Freebies.htm.

CURRICULAR BOARDS

This is my favorite type of board and one that I find is used least in most classrooms. Bulletin boards provide excellent opportunities to present material that you do not have time to study in the classroom curriculum. These postings could include different subjects of interest or related supplemental material.

For example, when I covered the United States Constitution, I posted a display of a special issue of *Life* magazine published in 1989. The theme of the issue was the Constitution's bicentennial. The magazine had information about the signers, a complete history of the document, examples of amendments that failed, and what life was like in the United States in the late eighteenth century. I purchased several copies of this issue and posted the material on the bulletin boards. All of it was information I would never have time to teach within the time constraints of the class. The articles were short, and the pictures were interesting. The students loved them and read the articles whenever they had free time.

With the advent of the No Child Left Behind Act and the emphasis on standardized testing, teachers have often come to the conclusion that it is virtually impossible to teach every substandard that is tested (see Mandel, 2006). Using curricular boards to post material is an excellent way to expose the students to tested material that you simply do not have time to cover in class. As a new teacher, however, you probably will not have enough familiarity with the end-of-the-year test to make these sorts of decisions. Therefore, it is imperative that you consult with veteran teachers in your grade level as to the tested areas that will most likely not be covered through your normal classroom curriculum.

Teacher Tool

Inspirational quotations are always useful to have on hand for philosophical boards or to write on the chalkboard. Numerous quotation collections exist, particularly online. Go to www.refdesk.com/factquot.html for a lengthy list of quotation Web sites. Bartleby.com is another excellent quotation source (including the full text of *Bartlett's Familiar Quotations*, which you can search by keyword).

SHOW-OFF BOARDS

By far the greatest use of bulletin boards, especially in the elementary grades, is to exhibit students' work, but this use can also be damaging to students' self-esteem—and the teacher is rarely aware of it. (See Chapter 10, "Discipline Issues," for a full discussion of the role of self-esteem in student behavior.)

When you post student work, do the following classroom self-esteem check: Look around the classroom at the displayed student work and count how many pieces are from students who are academically above average, average, and below average.

Then examine where the work of students in each category is displayed:

- How prominent is each piece in classroom? On the front wall? Back wall? Side?
- How is the work positioned? In the center of the display? On the outer edge?

Now determine how many of your students have no work displayed. How many have more than three items displayed?

A student's self-esteem can be influenced by something as simple as the student work chosen to be displayed on the classroom bulletin boards and the placement of this work. Student self-esteem will improve, and student work will therefore improve, if all students get an equal chance to see their work displayed prominently in the classroom.

One way of ensuring equal access of all your students to display opportunities is to keep a chart—independently in your roll book—noting each time a piece of student work is exhibited.

CONCLUDING THOUGHTS

Bulletin boards can be used in a number of different fashions beyond posting student work. They can set the tone of your class and provide the students with supplemental curricular material. Make the most of your bulletin boards by incorporating informational, philosophical, curricular, and show-off boards in your room throughout the year.

FOR FURTHER READING ON THIS SUBJECT

Hawthorne, K., & Gibson, J. E. (2002). *Bulletin board power: Bridges to lifelong learning.* Westport, CT: Libraries Unlimited.

Passatore, M. A. (1998). *Bulletin board? Or bulletin boards!* Landam, MD: Scarecrow Press.

Robbins, K., & Schmitt, L. (2002). *Big bulletin boards: A cooperative approach* (2nd ed.). Seattle, WA: Hide and Seek Press.

4

A Helpful Binder to Leave for Substitute Teachers

Aliya learned that she had to attend a teacher workshop for three days. Remembering what happened when a substitute teacher took over classes when she was a student, she became concerned with what might occur in her class during her three-day absence. She wondered what she could do to avert a potential disaster.*

Grade Levels

K–12

Timeline

Second week through the sixth week of school

The Issue

What can I do to prepare a substitute teacher for taking over my classroom?

*Basic ideas in this chapter contributed by Diane Clark, Townsend Central Public School, Waterford, Ontario, Canada.

THE IDEA

The one thing on which substitute teachers unanimously agree is that, to have a successful day, it is important to get acquainted with the classroom routines as quickly as possible.

Whenever I have the opportunity to contact the substitute before an absence, I review my procedures and lesson plan. I expect my classroom plans to be followed, and I expect learning to take place. I don't want my program to suffer if I have to be absent and need a substitute teacher.

Every September, I create a binder for any substitute teacher who may replace me temporarily. It means peace of mind for me and for the substitute.

The contents of the binder are as follows:

- An easy-to-follow table of contents for reference
- A letter of introduction to my classroom (I include both my home phone number and my cell phone number in case there are questions that cannot be answered by someone at the school)
- A list of the locations of all important reference materials, such as my roll book
- A copy of my basic class schedule and the school's various bell schedules
- A seating plan for each of my classes, with notes identifying students who can help, have special needs, or need special attention
- A map of the school with the appropriate offices and the staff rooms highlighted (such as the offices in charge of attendance, discipline, and health)
- A list of selected staff, and the subjects they teach, in case the substitute needs assistance with curriculum
- A brief explanation of the *do*s and *don't*s for the classroom, especially in the areas where the students most often try to manipulate the substitute teacher—be sure to provide examples
- Two emergency lessons for each of the subjects I teach, such as language arts, history, and geography (these keep from year to year; you can ask mentor teachers or department chairs if they have sample lessons)
- A set of curricular activities on which the class can work for the first ten to fifteen minutes of the morning or period, while the substitute teacher gets organized

Keep the binder on your desk and let the office staff and a student classroom helper know of its existence and location.

The contents of this binder serve to accompany a regular planning book (such as a lesson plan book), not replace it. Once you take the time to create the binder, the contents remain virtually the same each year except for the class lists, seating plans, and bell schedules. Substitute teachers really appreciate this information, and you can be away from class knowing that the substitute is well prepared.

> The one thing on which substitute teachers unanimously agree is that, to have a successful day, it is important to get acquainted with the classroom routines as quickly as possible.

Teacher Tool

You should also prepare your students for a day with a substitute teacher. Let them know your expectations—that your students are a reflection of your teaching, and that you expect their best behavior. Review with them what the substitute will be doing the following day in class, especially if it is different from your normal routine or lessons. This will lessen the tendency of students saying to the substitute teacher, "Our teacher doesn't do that. Instead, we should . . ." Remind them of the regular behavior expected in the class. Focus on areas where students often try to manipulate a substitute teacher, such as leaving the classroom to use the bathroom or get a drink of water when you normally would not allow it, or changing seats and working with friends.

CONCLUDING THOUGHTS

The more prepared the substitute teacher is, the more smoothly and efficiently your classroom will operate in your absence. A special substitute binder will greatly help the substitute in your classroom that day. Preparing your students for a day with a substitute teacher will also make the day go much more smoothly.

FOR FURTHER READING ON THIS SUBJECT

Mills, D. W. (Ed.). (2000). *Substitute teacher homepage: The substitute teacher survival site.* Retrieved February 23, 2009, from http://www.csrnet.org/csrnet/substitute.

Rude, C. A. (2007). *How to succeed as a substitute teacher: Everything you need from start to finish.* Thousand Oaks, CA; Corwin.

Smith, G. G., Latham, G., Longhurst, M. L., & Ditlevsen, M. (2004). *Substitute teacher handbook K–12* (6th ed.). Logan, UT: Substitute Teacher Workshop/Utah State University.

PART II

The Curriculum and the Students

✓ **Fairness and Critical Thinking in Classroom Discussions**

How can I treat students fairly in classroom discussions and get them to think critically?

✓ **Teaching Five Hours of Material in Only Three Hours**

How can I plan for teaching everything I am supposed to teach in a minimal amount of time?

✓ **Keeping Students Interested**

How can I be creative when teaching the material in my first year?

✓ **Teaching Test-Taking Skills**

How can I teach my students to succeed on tests?

✓ **The Internet as the Ultimate Teacher Resource Center**

How can I quickly and efficiently supplement my curriculum using the Internet?

✓ **Discipline Issues**

How can I prevent and alleviate discipline problems?

5

Fairness and Critical Thinking in Classroom Discussions

Aliya's mentor came in to observe her class. Although the evaluation was positive, the teacher noticed that Aliya always called on the same five or six students, who continually raised their hands during the classroom discussion. In addition, most of the questions she asked were low-level critical-thinking questions. How could she raise the level of her questions and involve additional students?

Grade Levels

K–12

Timeline

All year, but especially during the first two months of school as you become comfortable with your teaching

The Issue

How can I treat students fairly in classroom discussions and get them to think critically?

THE IDEA

There are two basic issues in questioning techniques:

- Fairness of questioning, involving all students equally
- Promoting the use of higher-order critical-thinking skills

FAIRNESS OF QUESTIONING

It is a natural reaction to call on the students who raise their hands to answer a question; however, it is most often the students with strong leadership personalities who consistently raise their hands. Conversely, those without strong leadership personalities rarely, if ever, raise their hands. (See the information on the leadership variable in Chapter 14, "Grading for Classroom Participation," for more information on these different personality types.)

As most teachers discover, a raised hand does not guarantee a correct answer. Furthermore, students don't always raise their hands when they know the correct answer. How do you give all students an equal chance to answer questions and participate in discussions?

> As most teachers discover, a raised hand does not guarantee a correct answer.

To ensure fairness, first establish a policy that in discussion, students do not raise their hands—you will call on everybody equally. There are three systems you can follow to guarantee this objective:

- Seating-pattern questioning
- Roll book–pattern questioning
- Organized chance questioning

Teacher Tool

One word of caution: Vary the pattern of your questioning every so often. The older the students, the quicker they will catch on and be able to predict whom you will call on next.

Seating-Pattern Questioning

Seating-pattern questioning is an easy method to use. Simply create a pattern in your mind, based on the seating arrangement, and call on the students according to your pattern. For example, you may call on every fourth student, or you may go back and forth from one side of the room to the other, in a set order. Once you have completed the entire pattern, you should have called on each student at least once.

Table 5.1   Roll Book–Pattern Questioning Example

Day of the Week When You Call on the Student	Last Name of Student
Monday	1 Acton
Tuesday	2 Aguilar
Wednesday	3 Baserio
Thursday	4 Bercelli
Friday	5 Cohen
Monday	6 Domatino
Tuesday	7 Dumas
Wednesday	8 Dyer
Thursday	9 Engler
Friday	10 Estarich

Roll Book–Pattern Questioning

Another way to make sure you call on everyone is to use your roll book to randomly select names of students. Most roll books are divided into groups of five. With your roll book open on your desk or front podium where you can glance at it, you call on the first person in each group of five on Monday, the second of each group on Tuesday, and so on. For example, on Monday, call on the students in the lines numbered 1, 6, 11, 16, 21, and 26. On Tuesday, call on those in lines numbered 2, 7, 12, 17, 22, and 27. (Remember to vary the pattern.) Eventually, you will get through the entire class and start over, having called on every student at least once. Of course, if you ask more questions than usual on a given day, simply move on to the next day's set of students. Table 5.1 illustrates this procedure.

Organized Chance Questioning

With organized chance, you simply ensure that in some fashion everyone will have an equal chance of being called on. For example, some teachers write the students' names on craft sticks and place them in a cup. Every time they need to call on someone, they take out a stick and call that name. The positive side of this system is that every student has an equal chance of being chosen, and there is no pattern the students can discover. To ensure you call on everyone equally, place all used sticks aside until the cup is empty. The negative side to this method is that it requires additional work for the teacher—creating the sticks, and stopping and starting each time the cup is empty—and secondary students may see the method as babyish.

Teacher Tool

Be sure that when you ask a question you pause long enough to provide "think time" before you call on a student. This allows all students a chance to cogitate on the question and keeps them all involved. New teachers tend to call on the first hands up and so the rest of the class disengages.

USE OF HIGHER-ORDER CRITICAL-THINKING SKILLS

Benjamin Bloom (1953) created a taxonomy to categorize the abstraction level of questions, starting with the most basic, lower-order thinking—knowledge—and ending with the most complex, higher-order thinking—evaluation. (See Table 5.2 for a summary of Bloom's taxonomy.) Studies have shown that students will respond using whatever critical-thinking level their teacher uses (see Mandel, 1991, 2003). Therefore, if you ask a question on a basic knowledge level, the students will

Table 5.2   Explanation of Bloom's Taxonomy

Question Level	Skills Students Will Demonstrate at Each Level
Knowledge	The ability to observe and recall information, including knowledge of details (such as dates, events, and places) and mastery of major ideas
Comprehension	The ability to comprehend information and meaning in a variety of contexts; the ability to compare, interpret, order, group, and understand cause and effect
Application	The ability to apply information, methods, and concepts, particularly to new situations and problem solving
Analysis	The ability to see the parts of a whole, including hidden meaning, and to recognize patterns
Synthesis	The ability to generalize based on facts, relate knowledge to various areas, draw conclusions and predict, and synthesize new ideas from established ones
Evaluation	The ability to discriminate among ideas and make choices and value judgments based on logical argument; the ability to recognize subjectivity

Table 5.3   Examples of Higher-Order Critical-Thinking Questions

A Discussion of the Civil War	
Application:	How did the North use their resources to give them an advantage in the war?
Analysis:	Why did the North have an advantage over the South?
Synthesis:	Using your knowledge of terrain, North and South strengths and weaknesses, and other factors, explain why the war ended the way it did.
Evaluation:	How did Grant's various strategies succeed in bringing about the end of the war?
A Discussion of the Story "The All-American Slurp"	
Application:	How did each member of the Chinese family apply his or her personality to learning English?
Analysis:	How do you think the Chinese mother, Mrs. Lin, felt about the American family's behavior at the dinner party?
Synthesis:	How do the different ethnic groups in our country contribute to a unique American culture?
Evaluation:	Which of the special customs of your culture, and your family, do you want to pass on to your children when you grow up?

respond with a knowledge-based answer. If you ask a synthesis-based question, the students will use synthesis in their responses.

To ensure you ask higher-order critical-thinking questions within each discussion, prepare a set of questions ahead of time. Often the textbook will include some. If you need additional questions, prepare them in advance using Bloom's taxonomy. Table 5.3 includes examples of higher-order questions in two contexts: a Civil War discussion and a short-story discussion.

Eventually, creating critical-thinking questions will become second nature. You can have the categories on paper right next to you and simply go through the list during every discussion.

CONCLUDING THOUGHTS

It is important to develop questioning techniques that ensure all students are called on equally. You can accomplish this by using seating patterns, your roll book, or organized chance. It is also important to ensure that classroom discussions incorporate higher-order critical-thinking questions, which you can accomplish by understanding Bloom's taxonomy and by preparing questions in advance.

FOR FURTHER READING ON THIS SUBJECT

Anderson, L. W., Krathwohl, D. R., Airasian, P. W., Cruikshank, K. A., Mayer, R. E., Pintrich, P. R., et al. (Eds.). (2000). *A taxonomy for learning, teaching, and assessing: A revision of Bloom's taxonomy of educational objectives, abridged edition* (2nd ed.). Columbus, OH: Allyn & Bacon.

Spiegel, D. L. (2005). *Classroom discussion: Strategies for engaging all students, building higher-level thinking skills, and strengthening reading and writing across the curriculum.* New York: Scholastic.

Walsh, J. A., & Sattes, B. D. (2004). *Quality questioning: Research-based practice to engage every learner.* Thousand Oaks: CA: Corwin.

6

Teaching Five Hours of Material in Only Three Hours

Aliya was frustrated. It was November, and according to her department guidelines, she was to be on Chapter 4 in the textbook. However, due to schedule interruptions, class changes, and just trying to get through what she had to do, she was only halfway through Chapter 3. How was she going to cover all of the required material in the time available?

Grade Levels

K–12

Timeline

All year, although it usually becomes most important beginning in the third month of school

The Issue

How can I plan for teaching everything I am supposed to teach in a minimal amount of time?

THE IDEA

Not having enough time to teach everything you are required to teach, or want to teach, is a common problem for all teachers. It is particularly problematic for the new teacher, who has not yet learned some of the tricks of delivering curriculum. Compounding the situation, many schools are now adopting prescribed reading and math programs that demand a set, significant time commitment or a pacing plan within the school day. In spite of this, there are things you can do to help fit the curriculum into the time provided:

- Integrate goals.
- Cover material through homework.
- Make choices.

INTEGRATE GOALS

There are two ways of integrating goals—within a subject area and across subject areas. Whether you can use one or both is dependent on your teaching situation.

Within Subject Areas

Whenever possible, combine and relate more than one curricular item or aspect with another. For example, in English, you can teach the skill of basic paragraph construction incorporating the comprehension exercises for a piece of literature. In math, you can teach related concepts such as fractions, decimals, percentages, and ratios together as much as possible. Too often these subjects are taught as complete individual units, yet they are interrelated and can be taught as such much more efficiently. Any teacher, in any teaching situation, can integrate goals within subject areas.

Across Subject Areas

The primary way to combine curricular goals is through the integration of subject areas. This is a rather easy process if you teach in a self-contained elementary class; it's a little more difficult in a secondary-school situation (unless, of course, you are teaching a two-period block, such as English and history or math and science, a trend in many middle schools). For example, English writing assignments can be about history or social studies topics; research papers can get a history grade for content and a separate English grade for usage and mechanics. Science experiments can be planned and scheduled according to the current math topic and vice versa.

You can also discover curricular combinations even when completely departmentalized, especially under the team concept when teachers essentially share the same students. With some

> Any teacher, in any teaching situation, can integrate goals within subject areas.

coordination, teachers can integrate their material with one another. For example, in grades when American history is taught, an English teacher can teach about persuasive essays using Thomas Paine's *Common Sense* at the same time as the history class is studying the American Revolution. Certain math concepts, such as graphing, can easily be taught by the science teacher. With advance planning, various curricular concepts can be taught simultaneously by teachers within the grade level, thereby reinforcing the material and making teaching more efficient.

COVER MATERIAL
THROUGH HOMEWORK

This is one of the most controversial but important ideas presented. Many people will insist that homework is only to be used to reinforce concepts taught in the classroom. Whereas reinforcement of concepts is the primary use of homework, I believe that much curricular material can be learned at home—and without parental or student frustration with new concepts.

Too many teachers believe homework to be nothing more than a review of the day's teaching. I disagree. If students can do ten division problems correctly in class, doing ten more at home is not going to further their abilities. The half-hour to an hour that they would spend on those problems, however, can be equivalent to an extra class period for covering additional curricular material.

Homework should be used not only for review, but to practice new concepts and to cover new subject matter. When the material is introduced in class and the students understand the task assigned, homework can be used, just as class time is, for basic practice on important curricular material. Larger assignments can be assigned and spread over two or three days (thereby also giving the students the opportunity to learn and practice time-management skills).

Please note, I am not advocating learning brand-new concepts or procedures at home. Rather, if a learning or study pattern is already established in class, the same processes can be continued at home. For instance, if a history chapter is divided into four sections with questions, instead of doing all of them in class, cover three in class and assign one for homework over a couple of days. The students already know how to comprehend a history chapter and what is expected with the subsequent questions. However, by having them read and complete one section at home, you will automatically cut class time on this chapter by 25%. All of the material—both from homework and class work—can be graded as you would grade any other curricular assignment.

You need to be aware of not giving students too much to do (every class and age can handle varying workloads), and to allow for those students who have comprehension problems. Still, rather than giving busywork for homework, or assigning homework for homework's sake, you can use the time to help cover curriculum that you cannot get to in class.

MAKE CHOICES

Prioritize what you feel is critical for the students to learn, what should be touched upon so the students recognize the material, and what you will teach if you have enough time. It's always better to teach the important material well rather than rush through everything, teaching nothing adequately.

How do you choose? Many districts are incorporating *power standards*, which are considered the most important state and district standards for students to master and are given priority over all other curricula. Aside from imposed standards, your priorities are often determined by what you teach. If you teach English or math, talk to teachers in the next grade level to see what are the most basic concepts that the students need to master before being promoted to the next class. For example, a fourth-grade math teacher may consider it critical that the students know their multiplication tables to twelve, the basic concept of fractions, and decimals to the hundredth place. The teacher may state that prior geometry knowledge isn't as important. (See Mandel, 2006, pp. 2–12, for an explanation as to how to prioritize curricula.)

If this is your first time using a particular textbook, look at the expectations for students at the end of the unit (see the unit assessment). This can assist you in determining what can be cut and what is essential information that must be taught.

Teacher Tool

Don't forget to use your curricular bulletin boards (see Chapter 3, "Bulletin Boards") to display supplemental material that isn't your top priority but that you want students to learn. The bulletin board is also an excellent tool for providing more detail and depth for those subjects you do consider a priority.

Knowing what the fourth-grade math teacher considers critical can guide you, a third-grade teacher, in your decisions about what to concentrate on in math. The same is true for English usage skills needed from one grade to another.

If you teach history, the subject usually will not be covered again for three or four years, so you will not be teaching prerequisite knowledge for the following grade. You can pick and choose what is really important, taking into account basic state and district standards. For example, if your history book has twelve chapters, select the nine most important—the ones that you will spend considerable time in covering. Don't skip the others entirely, but review them quickly, such as by having the students read the material and discuss it orally in class—no written questions, no test. In this fashion, they still are exposed to the material, and you have the time to go into depth in the most important areas. To assist in the choosing process, you can consult with your department chair, a mentor teacher, or your administrator. For example, Table 6.1 lists the units assigned to a sixth-grade history curriculum and how each one is taught, demonstrating this priority system.

Table 6.1   Prioritizing a Sixth-Grade History Curriculum

Unit	How It Is Prioritized
Early humans	Covered in detail and formally assessed
Mesopotamia	Covered in detail and formally assessed
Egypt and Kush	Covered in detail and formally assessed
Mesoamerica	Students are exposed to unit, no formal assessment; subject covered again in seventh-grade history book
Ancient Hebrews	Covered in detail and formally assessed
Ancient China	Covered in detail and formally assessed
Ancient India	Students are exposed to unit, no formal assessment; very little of this chapter is assessed on spring standardized exam
Ancient Greece	Covered in detail and formally assessed
Classical Greece	Covered in detail and formally assessed
Ancient Rome	Covered in detail and formally assessed
Roman republic	Covered in detail and formally assessed
Fall of Rome	Students are exposed to unit, no formal assessment; seventh-grade curriculum starts with this unit

By prioritizing these units, the sixth-grade history teacher can cover all of the important areas by the end of the year, rather than running out of time or teaching less than is required due to time constraints.

CONCLUDING THOUGHTS

Teachers don't have time to cover all the material that they are supposed to teach. This is especially true when prescribed reading or math programs are in place, or when a pacing plan is mandated. You need to make decisions on how to combine curricula, use homework more efficiently, and make curricular choices as to what's most important for students to learn.

FOR FURTHER READING ON THIS SUBJECT

Kiewra, K. A. (2008). *Teaching how to learn: The teacher's guide to student success.* Thousand Oaks, CA: Corwin.

Mandel, S. (2006). *Improving test scores: A practical approach for teachers and administrators.* Thousand Oaks, CA: Corwin.

Wolfe, S. (2006). *Your best year yet! A guide to purposeful planning and effective classroom organization.* Washington, DC: Teaching Strategies.

7

Keeping Students Interested

A liya gave the students a worksheet. Collectively the students moaned, and individuals called out, "Not another worksheet!" She was perplexed. The material was new; they hadn't seen it before, but she had used worksheets for student practice in every chapter. She was in a rut. She was a new teacher just learning how to teach this particular material. How could she be creative and keep her students interested?

Grade Levels

K–12

Timeline

All year, although you should concentrate on this topic by the third month especially, as you become comfortable with teaching

The Issue

How can I be creative when teaching the material in my first year?

THE IDEA

When you are attempting to get through the required material during your first year, trying to be creative may not seem important. However, a little creativity will help your lessons be successful, and most important, will keep your students engaged. Interested students do not disrupt the class very often.

The basic premise of creativity is *do it differently.*

It is important to vary your approach whenever possible. The following approaches can assist you:

- Incorporating the multiple intelligences
- Creative review

INCORPORATING THE MULTIPLE INTELLIGENCES

Multiple intelligence (MI) theory is a great guideline for ensuring that you use a variety of activities. (See Armstrong, 2000, for an excellent teacher guide to the multiple intelligences.) During the planning of each unit, review the intelligences to see if you are enabling students to use them, especially during student practice sessions. Besides the intellectual value of incorporating MI theory into your lessons, doing so ensures that you are using more varied and creative approaches.

> Interested students do not disrupt the class very often.

Of course, time constraints make it virtually impossible to do activities that focus on every intelligence for every topic you cover; however, within every unit, you may be able to use various activities creatively to target each of the intelligences at least once. Table 7.1 gives examples of the four core subject areas. Many of the ideas can be used from one subject area to another, simply changing the curricular content.

CREATIVE REVIEW

When reviewing material, such as before a test or at the end of a long assignment or chapter, be creative. For example, create a game out of the material, such as a *Jeopardy*-like game, where the students are given various categories, you provide the answers, and the students ask the corresponding question. The activity is fun, different, and covers the same review normally conducted in class. Keep the categories and answers to reuse whenever you teach that same material.

You can also make up games for the students to use in a review, such as video games that you draw on the board. Go to arcades, or question your students, to find out what games are popular and how they work. For example, you can draw a level of *Super Mario Brothers* and have the questions lead to prizes that the characters acquire by answering correctly. Each prize carries a separate point total depending on degree of difficulty.

Another idea is to use the Internet to find creative activities for student review or practice sessions. For example, there are Web sites that provide math story

Table 7.1   Using the Multiple Intelligences to Vary Instruction: The Four Core Subjects

English: A Short Story/Novel Example	
Intelligence	*Possible Supplemental Activity*
Verbal/linguistic	Write an original poem.
Logical/mathematical	Create a chart showing the progression of the story from exposition to rising action to the climax to the denouement. Also show where the external and internal conflicts arise.
Visual/spatial	Create a movie poster for a movie version of the story.
Bodily/kinesthetic	Act out a scene from the story.
Musical/rhythmic	Find a "theme song" for a character in the story.
Interpersonal	In a cooperative work group, discuss a potential sequel to the story.
Intrapersonal	Create a diary for one of the characters.
Naturalist	Discuss the setting of the story.
Math: An Equations Example	
Intelligence	*Possible Supplemental Activity*
Verbal/linguistic	Write out the procedures for solving multiple step equations.
Logical/mathematical	Using the board, go through the steps in solving the equation.
Visual/spatial	Draw pictures of balancing—both sides of an equation.
Bodily/kinesthetic	Using students, "act out" equations.
Musical/rhythmic	Discuss instrumentation of a piece of music, showing how each individual piece contributes to the whole.
Interpersonal	Create a cooperative learning game for solving multiple-step equations.
Intrapersonal	Work on personal puzzles at home working out equations.
Naturalist	Create equations in nature, and discuss what happens when things are removed or introduced.
History: A Civil War Example	
Intelligence	*Possible Supplemental Activity*
Verbal/linguistic	Pretend you are a politician during the war and write a short speech to Congress from the perspective of the North or the South.

(Continued)

Table 7.1 (Continued)

Intelligence	Possible Supplemental Activity
Logical/mathematical	Create a flow chart showing how one event led to another in bringing about the Civil War.
Visual/spatial	Create a poster with slogans or information to promote the North or the South position.
Bodily/kinesthetic	Create an improvisational scene about a border-state family debating whether they should support a war, and if so, which side.
Musical/rhythmic	Rewrite the lyrics to a popular song, explaining one of the positions of the Civil War.
Interpersonal	Working in pairs or groups of three, prepare a five-minute presentation on one aspect of the Civil War for the class.
Intrapersonal	Write an individual journal entry, taking the role of someone living at that time and discussing the causes of the war, what you plan to do, and why.
Naturalist	Describe how the terrain and weather may have affected the outcome of various Civil War battles.
Science: A Life Cycle of Animals Example	
Intelligence	Possible Supplemental Activity
Verbal/linguistic	Read a short story concerning an animal, i.e. *Rikki-Tikki-Tavi* or *Charlotte's Web*.
Logical/mathematical	Chart out how one stage of the life cycle leads into another.
Visual/spatial	Create pictures of various stages of the life cycle.
Bodily/kinesthetic	Act out examples of various parts of the life cycle.
Musical/rhythmic	Listen to a selections of songs about animals.
Interpersonal	Have cooperative work groups select and research the life cycle of various animals with the goal of creating the perfect zoological habitat for the animals.
Intrapersonal	Individual research for the above project.
Naturalist	Keep and raise a class animal, watching the life cycle.

problems using the characters from the popular Harry Potter series. You can also locate Web sites to create crossword puzzles (a great review opportunity) or other types of puzzles you can design with your curricula (locating supplemental material on the Internet is reviewed in Chapter 9).

Many of these and other items can go into an "anchor" or extra credit box. You can include worksheets that are fun but still challenging using higher-order critical-thinking skills. These can include logic types of problems, thinking games, and other material that will interest your students and get them to think.

CONCLUDING THOUGHTS

It is important not to get into a rut—students thrive on novelty. Be creative with your curricular review techniques and incorporate the multiple intelligences into your teaching. Be sure to vary your teaching approaches as well, especially during student practice or review sessions.

FOR FURTHER READING ON THIS SUBJECT

Evanski, G. A. (2008). *Classroom activities: More than 100 ways to energize learners* (2nd ed.). Thousand Oaks, CA: Corwin.

Mandel, S. (2003). *Cooperative work groups: Preparing students for the real world.* Thousand Oaks, CA: Corwin.

Turville, J. (2007). *Differentiating by student interest: Strategies and lesson plans.* Larchmont, NY: Eye on Education.

8

Teaching Test-Taking Skills

Aliya's students were not doing well on their tests. They seemed to understand the material and the concepts, as was evident in their class work and discussions. When asked, they insisted that they were studying for the tests. She didn't know whether their study habits or the tests were the problem.

> **Grade Levels**
>
> 3–12
>
> **Timeline**
>
> The first month of school, starting with your first major test
>
> **The Issue**
>
> How can I teach my students to succeed on tests?

THE IDEA

Test taking is a skill, and it is one of the most important ones that your students can learn. However you may feel about the process, tests are embedded in our society. Like it or not, in this age of No Child Left Behind (NCLB)—be it end-of-the-year or periodic exams—standardized testing is the primary vehicle used for evaluation of all educational institutions and personnel. On a personal note for the students, the SAT and ACT tests are still critical for getting into most universities. Test taking is a skill that is critical for student success.

You can and should teach students how to study well for a test. Contrary to what they may believe, testing success is a question of *quality* study time versus *quantity* of study time. Students must be convinced that this is for their benefit, not yours. As much as they may protest, arguments that may have an effect on them are the following:

- "How do you feel when you bring home a good test score?"
- "How can you avoid what happens when you bring home a bad test score?"
- "Do you enjoy spending five hours studying for a test and only earning a C, or would you like to learn how to study for three hours and receive an A or B?"

Once students are convinced that you can help them get better grades, review the following topics with them:

- How *not* to study
- Using flash cards
- Reviewing the book's concepts, not just the words
- Creating a study environment

HOW *NOT* TO STUDY

The primary way that students study is by reading the assigned chapter or other materials a couple of times. This is also one of the worst ways to study. To illustrate: When you watch a television rerun, do you do other things? Probably yes. Do you fully concentrate? Probably not. The reason? You've seen it before, and you know what's coming.

The same concept applies to studying. When a student reads a chapter more than once, her mind already has an idea of what is next, what is on the bottom of the page, or even what is on the next page. The result is that the mind begins to wander and concentration diminishes. Therefore, central to effective studying is to review the material in new and different ways, thereby keeping the brain at attention.

USING FLASH CARDS

Flash cards are probably the single most important tool that a student can use in studying. Students can create cards of key terms, concepts, formulas—virtually any information that may appear on the test. Be sure to demonstrate to the students what are and where to find the key terms, concepts, and formulas relevant to your curriculum. Often they will have no idea how to evaluate this information.

By using flash cards, the students reinforce and study the material in two different ways. First, during the actual creation of the flash cards, the student is slowly and deliberately reviewing each piece of information while writing the question

> Central to effective studying is to review the material in new and different ways, thereby keeping the brain at attention.

or concept on the front of the card and the answer or explanation on the back. Second, as the student shuffles and reads the cards, the material is presented in a new order each time, thereby keeping it fresh.

REVIEWING THE BOOK'S CONCEPTS, NOT JUST THE WORDS

Besides using flash cards, students need to learn the basic concepts being presented rather than simply rereading the material. This can be accomplished in a number of ways.

First, the student should review all study questions presented by the author, including those written in the margins or at the beginning or end of sections and chapters. If the student has already answered them and had them evaluated, he should correct and study incorrect answers. Chances are, more often than not, those questions will lead to the specific information asked on the test.

The student must also review all pictures, charts, maps, and graphs included in the chapter and ask, "Why are they there?" These materials are not in the book because they are pretty. They are there because they exemplify specific concepts in the chapter. The student needs to be able to identify and understand those concepts, for they are sure to show up on the test.

CREATING A STUDY ENVIRONMENT

This is probably the most difficult process for students to accept, and it is one of their biggest obstacles to succeeding on tests. In creating a study environment, distractions need to be at a minimum. This includes the television, telephone, iPods, video games, and often siblings. Music, if necessary (such as for those with a strong musical intelligence), should be low and without distracting words. The student should be comfortable, but not so comfortable that her mind wanders. Sitting at a desk or table—the actual test-taking environment—is preferable to lying down on a bed.

Students should limit their study time to no more than forty-five minutes to an hour in one sitting. After that, they need to either take a fifteen- to thirty-minute break or move on to something else and come back to the study material. After forty-five to sixty minutes of total concentration, the second hour of studying is much less effective. The brain requires rest. Students can study three to four hours for a test, but they must take regular mental breaks throughout the study period. They need to learn that rehearsal is crucial to learning information for a test. It is better to study for a shorter time over several nights than at one long sitting. Pacing is the key, a concept difficult for many students to learn.

Finally, each student should develop a plan for studying, a short to-do list of the areas to study during one evening. He then checks off each area as it is accomplished; this action gives the student positive internal reinforcement. See Figure 8.1 for an example.

Figure 8.1   A Studying Checklist

Make copies of this page, and go through this checklist every time you have a major test. No one has to see this but you! As you go through it, you will find that your studying is more organized and (surprisingly) you begin to get better grades on your tests (which will make you and, it is to be hoped, your parents happy).

_____ Set up a quiet place to study (table or desk, chair).

_____ Make flash cards of all key terms and concepts. Go over the cards so you get each one correct at least once.

_____ Go over textbook review questions, pages _____.

_____ Review all textbook pictures, maps, graphs and charts. List pages to key in on

_____.

STUDY SCHEDULE

Plan out your study schedule and cross out as you go through it.

_____ START TIME

_____ BREAK TIME (45–90 minutes after start time, depending on the subject)

_____ START TIME

_____ BREAK TIME

_____ START TIME

_____ BREAK TIME

_____ START TIME

CONCLUDING THOUGHTS

In this age of NCLB, test taking is even more a critical skill to success in school than before. You need to teach good test-taking skills. This includes teaching the students how not to study, how to use flash cards, how to review the book's concepts (rather than just the words), and how to create a good study environment.

> **Teacher Tool**
>
> You may need to work with students who share a room with a sibling and have no suitable study area. Investigate alternatives, such as a local library, study places on campus, or a friend's house.

FOR FURTHER READING ON THIS SUBJECT

Mandel, S. (2006). *Improving test scores: A practical approach for teachers and administrators.* Thousand Oaks, CA: Corwin.

Peltz, W. H. (2007). *Dear teacher: Expert advice for effective study skills.* Thousand Oaks, CA: Corwin.

Rozakis, L. (2002). *Super study skills.* New York: Scholastic.

9

The Internet as the Ultimate Teacher Resource Center

Aliya was starting a new unit and needed supplemental materials, but her school's materials were limited. She had heard over and over again that teachers were expected to use their own money to purchase supplementary educational items. She looked at her checkbook and was not happy. There was a limit to what she could spend out of her own pocket. How could she provide the curriculum she needed to her students without depleting her bank account?

Grade Levels

K–12

Timeline

All year, but especially when planning your first major curricular unit

The Issue

How can I quickly and efficiently supplement my curriculum using the Internet?

THE IDEA

This chapter has nothing to do with putting your students on the Internet. Rather, it is meant as a way to demonstrate how the Internet is truly the ultimate teacher resource center. The Internet can supply you with endless no-cost, quality supplemental materials. All you need to know is where to look and how to retrieve them. The Internet can be used as a resource for holiday art projects for primary students; math story problems using current cartoon characters for upper elementary students; and primary source material for secondary classes, particularly history. The possibilities are infinite. The biggest problem is the time it takes to locate useable Web sites. Using search engines or directories can be a long and inefficient process. You have to sort through numerous useless sites, and many of the best educational sites are not even listed. There are some cybertools, however, that can significantly quicken your search and provide you with the results you need.

There are thousands of books on using the Internet. Unfortunately, some of the least useful are those that provide you with the "hundred best sites." Very often these sites no longer work, or worse, you will feel a reluctance to take the time to go through the book.

However, there are excellent useful sites, which are considered "portals." These are sites that will directly lead you to hundreds of other sites. If you follow link to link, you can find virtually any curricular material you want—and all without remembering or typing in a URL.

Portals consist of a number of different types of Web sites that you should bookmark on your personal computer. These are major educational locations, which can quickly and efficiently direct you to whatever you may be looking for within minutes, sometimes seconds. Once there, you print out the relevant material and bring it into class, directly integrating it into your curriculum.

Teacher Tool

Be sure to check your state's acceptable use/fair use policy for using published material. It is generally acceptable to copy a portion (less than a chapter, for example) of a printed copyrighted work if your use is educational only, and for your classroom only. The same concept has recently been applied to works on the Internet.

The key to efficient use of the Internet is to have places already set up where you can begin looking for specific material. These are sites where you know you can go in order to link to other sites that will then get you to the information you need.

The most important site to have on your computer is a general education Web site. This type of site provides you with links to a number of other important locations, including those described in the box at the end of this chapter. A site such as Teachers Helping Teachers (www.pacificnet.net/~mandel) will supply general Web sites in every subject matter (scroll down and click on the "educational resources" link). When you use a general education Web site, you no longer have to remember URLs or keep lists of addresses. From this one site, you can eventually get to anything you want.

There is a general subject matter Web site for every major subject. These sites provide links to dozens of additional sites in their area. You should find one that you like within your subject area, bookmark it, and refer to it at the beginning of every new unit or chapter. Some examples are in the box at the end of this chapter. You can find all of these linked from the "Educational Resources" page of Teachers Helping Teachers.

One more type of site that you should be aware of is a good teacher guest book, such as the one located on Teachers Helping Teachers. In this guest book, you can ask questions, make requests, or simply share your problems with other teachers online throughout the world. Follow the directions and expect two to eight answers, by e-mail, within 72 hours.

CONCLUDING THOUGHTS

Most schools have limited budgets for supplemental curricular materials. Rather than spending your own money, you can use the Internet. Through the use of general education Web sites, general subject matter Web sites, and teacher guest books, within minutes you will find virtually any supplemental curricular material you need.

Subject Area Web Sites

Reading and Language Arts: The Children's Literature Web Guide (www.ucalgary.ca/~dkbrown/index.html) has a lot of information about every facet of children's literature. Be sure to look at the link to "Authors on the Web," which will provide you with Web sites for almost every children's author whose work you may use. By using this site, you can bring in plenty of supplemental material for the study of any novel or story in your curriculum.

Math: The Math Forum @Drexel (www.mathforum.org) provides links and materials for virtually every area of K–12 math. Click on "resources and tools" then "math tools." Use the pull-down menus on top for additional links organized by grade level, math subject, or type of resource. The student center and teacher center are also valuable areas of this site.

History and Social Studies: An excellent history and social studies site is called Best of History Web Sites (www.besthistorysites.net). This site contains thousands of links to educational sites. Depending on your history or social studies theme, you might link to "Medieval History," "Early European History," or "American History." Once at the subject page, select the appropriate category and scan the hundreds of sites offered for your use.

Science: A science teacher in San Francisco organized Cody's Science Education Zone (www.tlc.ousd.k12.ca.us/~acody). Click on "Links" for a listing of the best science sites available. From those sites, you can access any subject area.

The Arts: The World Wide Arts Resource (www.wwar.com) will direct you to material in most areas related to the arts. For example, click on "browse the arts" at the bottom of the homepage, then click on "Famous Artists/Art History Artists" and you will find links to Web sites devoted to hundreds of famous artists, sites from which you can download numerous examples of their work to share with your students. (Color ink-jet printers, with good quality reproduction, now sell for less than $50.)

These are some basic examples of subject matter Internet sites to use for securing supplemental curricular materials. You may locate others you like better—new ones continually become established. The key is to know where they are, to evaluate their quality, and to use them to supplement your curriculum without using your own money.

FOR FURTHER READING ON THIS SUBJECT

Ebiefung, A. (2002). *Responsible use of the Internet in education: Issues concerning evaluation, citation, copyright and fair use of web materials.* Cleveland, TN: Penman.

Mandel, S. (2003). *Cooperative work groups: Preparing students for the real world.* Thousand Oaks, CA: Corwin.

Nelson, K. J. (2007). *Teaching in the digital age: Using the Internet to increase student engagement and understanding* (2nd ed.). Thousand Oaks, CA: Corwin.

10

Discipline Issues

Aliya had one male student who constantly disrupted the class. When she would discipline him, he would always argue and eventually escalate the situation until he would get into more trouble than the original disruption warranted. Worse than that, he ruined her day. She was upset for at least the next hour or two. She didn't know how to rectify this situation.

Grade Levels

K–12

Timeline

All year, but especially the first couple weeks of school

The Issue

How can I prevent and alleviate discipline problems?

THE IDEA

We all know how important discipline is in the classroom, and you may be wondering why this chapter is the last of this section. The fact is, if you do the rest of the ideas in this and the previous chapters, your discipline problems will be at a minimum.

Still, discipline issues are probably the greatest concern of all new teachers. New teachers want to know what to do, when to do it, and how to do it, and they would like one specific rule that will address all of their problems.

Well, here is the number one rule for good discipline:

There is no rule.

Every teacher is unique; every student is unique; every situation is unique. What works with one student may not work with another; what worked at 10 a.m. may not work at 2 p.m. So what do you do?

There are no procedures or methods to alleviate all discipline problems, but there are ten basic principles you can apply in virtually every situation. These are central to teaching and central to your classroom success. The following ten principles, which are in no particular order, are of equal importance:

> There are no procedures or methods to alleviate all discipline problems, but there are ten basic principles you can apply in virtually every situation.

You Must Have Control

This does not mean be a dictator. It means you determine what occurs in the class. *You*, not the students, set the tone. You determine the positive and negative consequences. Even if you run a democratic classroom, you are the one giving the students the power they have, as you are the one to limit it. Do not be afraid to exercise your power when needed. This leads to the next principle:

You Are Their Teacher, Not Their Friend

You can be friendly with your students, but there must be a boundary you do not cross. You are the adult and not their peer. Review your own career as a student. Which teachers did you like the best? Which did you have the most respect for? Generally it won't be those who wanted to be friends with their students. You can and should, however, demonstrate to the students that you genuinely care about them and that, like a parent, what you do is ultimately for their benefit.

Behavior Is the Problem, Not the Student

When responding to a discipline issue, concentrate on the inappropriate behavior, not on the student. When discussing the issue, be objective and descriptive. State, for example, "You called out in a loud voice three times this period already." This type of statement focuses on a specific student behavior. Avoid saying things such as "You have no respect," or "You're always disrupting my class." These types of statements suggest that the student is basically bad.

In addition, when the negative behavior ends, consider the issue over and don't continually reference it. For example, in an elementary school, when students are given a time-out in the classroom, inform them that when they can act appropriately, they can return to their seats. Very often, within fifteen minutes or so, a student will return to his or her seat and behave well. While in time-out, if the student raises a hand to participate in a class discussion, make a point to call on him or her. In a secondary school, when a student returns from the referral room, do not remind him or her of the negative behaviors. Do not threaten that if the behavior is repeated, he or she will be sent out once more. Instead, welcome the student back and keep the past in the past.

Whenever possible, remind the students that it is certain behaviors you don't like and that you do like them as people. This leads to the next principle:

Discover the Source of the Problem

Contrary to public opinion, there's no such thing as a bad kid. Students do not wake up in the morning and rub their hands together in glee, saying, "What can I do today to disrupt the class?" They act up for a reason. You need to discover that reason. When you accomplish that, you are on your way to solving most of your discipline problems. The following are common reasons for bad behavior:

- *Boredom:* This is, more often than not, the reason for disruptions. During discipline and classroom management workshops, I ask the teachers what is the major reason for disruptions in the class. Initially and inevitably the blame is placed on the students, their parents, or their environment. Then someone eventually mentions that the student is bored, which places the responsibility directly on the teacher. Boredom can be an issue with gifted kids in particular. This may or may not always be the reason, but it's the first place to look.
- *Personal Family Problems:* Often a student acts out because of problems at home. If there was a major fight that morning in the house, or on the way to school, it may affect a student the entire day. To resolve the problem, talk to the student privately. You may get an answer, or you may not. Either way, if a personal family issue is the cause of the student's negative behavior, you can address the behavior from a different perspective. (Be sure to eliminate child abuse or neglect as causes. If they are, follow the guidelines for reporting as determined by your district.)
- *Girlfriend/Boyfriend Problems:* This situation is acute in fifth to seventh grade. When a problem develops that was not there before in a sixth-grade class, the first question I ask is, "Who broke up with whom?" or "Who's mad at whom today?" At that point, you can choose to ignore the problem, arrange for them to work it out, or inform them of the consequences if the behavior continues.
- *Student Did Not Take Medication:* This problem happens often with elementary and sometimes with middle school students. Be aware if you have students taking medication, especially for attention deficit disorder (ADD) or attention deficit hyperactivity disorder (ADHD). Privately ask if the student has taken his or her medication that day. If not, do not discipline the child. He or she does not have control and really should not be punished for the behavior. Send the student to the health office, requesting that he or she

call home to get the medication. (See Chapter 20, "Students With ADD/ADHD and Classroom Management," for more information.)

- *Full Moon:* This is not a joke. Elementary teachers can often tell when it's a full moon without looking outside. Windy days also cause strange reactions from these students. Sometimes there is no rhyme or reason for certain behaviors.

Be Fair

Being fair is critical. Students will accept negative consequences, even if they don't like them, if they know the consequences are fair. There must be equal treatment—within reason. If not, you need to be able to, and should, justify your action. If you can't justify it, do not do it, for you will immediately lose the students' respect, and then the problems will really begin.

For example, when a student hits another student, discipline both of the students. When questioned "why," ask the student who was hit what he or she did to provoke the other student. There will always be a reason. Ask, "If you had not done _____, would you have gotten hit?" The "no" answer provides the justification to discipline both. The students immediately see your fairness, and you consequently earn their respect.

Be Consistent

Consistency is also important. Students need to know how you will act in most situations. They need to know your limits to adjust their own behaviors to stay within your limits. This is not a question of whether to be strict or lax. It is a matter of establishing guidelines and expectations. Think of some of your strictest or hardest teachers. They may have been difficult, but you knew where they stood and where their limits were.

Don't Show Negative Emotion

Often the only control that students have is over your emotions. If a student is embarrassed in front of his or her peers because of the negative consequences issued by the teacher, the student often tries to save face. This is especially the case with students in fifth grade or older. Think about it: When students are caught doing something inappropriate, they know they were caught, they know the probable consequences, and they know what will or will not happen if they argue with you. So why do they still argue? It's because they reason that if they're going down, they're going to bring you down too and ruin your day. Don't allow a student to get you visibly upset and walk out of the room with a victorious smile.

The solution? Control your negative emotions. You are the adult. Do not allow your buttons to be pushed. Smile. You may be seething inside, but do everything in your power not to display it. When you don't react, it is not worth students' time or effort to argue or upset you. If their actions only result in further trouble, what's the sense in doing them?

Learn to Ignore

One of the important skills you can develop is learning when to ignore negative behaviors. Students may do something they are aware will cause a reaction, but not something important enough to get them into trouble. The best response is simply to ignore the behavior. If it is not disrupting the class, ignore it. More often than not, the behavior will go away by itself. (Obviously, if the behavior escalates to where it disrupts the class, you cannot ignore it.)

Often simply standing near the student will extinguish the behavior—the student is aware you know what's going on, but you're giving one more chance to change the behavior before you act.

Be Human

One way you get respect from the students is to show them that you are human. When you are wrong (and you will be), admit it, change your decision, and apologize if necessary. You will earn respect for showing how fair you are. If you are not feeling well, or are having a bad day (as they may have at times), inform your class ahead of time. You'll be surprised at the understanding and respect this will engender. This is connected to the last principle:

Use Your Own Style—Don't Copy Others

You need to be yourself. You cannot use only the directions and techniques of others. You cannot pick up a discipline book and follow its concrete everyday ideas to the letter. It is not natural, nor will it be you. Do what you feel is right. Remember these ten principles and adapt them to your particular teaching situation and to your particular students.

When you are comfortable with your classroom management, when you follow basic principles of how to best run your classroom, you may not need to worry about discipline problems.

You won't have any.

Teacher Tool

With the advent of the student Internet use, along with their fascination with texting one another, a new problem has begun to arise—cyberbullying. As it is a new problem, educators are just now trying to figure out how to deal with it. Some districts feel that what happens between students outside of the school is none of their business. Others have the opposite view. If you suspect cyberbullying among your students, check with your school administrator as to the school's policy for dealing with the matter. You can also consult the new book, *Bullying Beyond the Schoolyard: Preventing and Responding to Cyberbullying*, by Sameer Hinduja and Justin W. Patchin, 2008, Corwin.

CONCLUDING THOUGHTS

Contrary to new teachers' desires, there is no one rule for good discipline. Every teacher is unique, every class is unique, every situation is unique. What works on Tuesday may not work Thursday. However, there are basic principles for discipline every teacher can use. These include keeping control of your class; acting like their teacher, not like a friend; and realizing that the specific behavior is the problem, not the students themselves. In addition, if you work on discovering the actual source of a problem, being fair and consistent, not showing negative emotion, being human, learning when and how to ignore behavior, and using your own style, you'll have fun in the classroom.

FOR FURTHER READING ON THIS SUBJECT

Burke, K. (2008). *What to do with the kid who . . . : Developing cooperation, self-discipline, and responsibility in the classroom.* Thousand Oaks, CA: Corwin.

Nelson, J., Lott, L., & Glenn, H. S. (2000). *Positive discipline in the classroom: Developing mutual respect, cooperation, and responsibility in your classroom* (Rev. 3rd ed.). New York: Three Rivers Press.

Smith, R. (2008). *Conscious classroom management: Unlocking the secrets of great teaching* (3rd ed.). Thousand Oaks, CA: Corwin.

PART III

Grading

✓ **Marking Papers and Promoting Self-Esteem**

How can I grade papers and keep the students' self-esteem high at the same time?

✓ **A Beginner's Guide to Figuring Grades**

What is the easiest, most efficient, and fairest way to determine my students' grades?

✓ **Rubrics**

How can I create a rubric that is valid and fair?

✓ **Grading for Classroom Participation**

Should I grade classroom participation?

✓ **A Student Self-Esteem Check**

How can I verify that self-esteem is being fostered in my classroom environment?

11

Marking Papers and Promoting Self-Esteem

Aliya was always concerned about her students' self-esteem. It hurt her to see the downcast looks on their faces whenever she returned papers full of red marks. But what options did she have? She had to give them the grades they earned. She wondered what she could do to raise their self-esteem and at the same time give them appropriate feedback on their papers.

Grade Levels

K–12

Timeline

All year, starting with your first graded assignment

The Issue

How can I grade papers and keep the students' self-esteem high at the same time?

THE IDEA

Many of the things teachers do to promote or inhibit self-esteem come from unintended actions. There are obvious things teachers do that overtly affect self-esteem, such as whom they call on in class and whose papers they display on the bulletin boards. However, a teacher has a greater impact on students through less obvious actions that directly affect the students' self-esteem, such as when evaluating student papers.

Following are some quick tips that any teacher can immediately use in improving the self-esteem in the class, while still maintaining credibility in marking papers:

- Never grade in red ink. Use green or blue ink.
- Use a slash rather than an X to mark a wrong answer.
- Indicate the number of correct answers instead of subtracting the number wrong.

NEVER GRADE IN RED INK

In American society, and in most societies, red is considered a negative color. In our society, it is used on stop signs and lights, warning labels, poison, to indicate the devil, and so forth. If you see a red light, you naturally hesitate. We are conditioned to view the color red as something negative, or at least prohibitive.

A paper that is handed back full of red marks conveys to the student, often subconsciously, that there is something wrong with him or her intellectually. This can lead to a self-fulfilling prophecy, with the student lowering his or her own expectations and subsequent work quality.

Green is a positive color in our society, and to a lesser degree, so is blue. When you see a green light, you give it little concern or attention—you subconsciously know that there is no problem, that everything is all right.

In the students' eyes, teacher corrections or markings in green ink come across as constructive criticism. There is little negative social stigma attached as there is with the color red. Even though two papers may contain the identical number of answers marked as incorrect, the paper with green marks will not trigger the immediate negative feelings that the one with red marks will. Other colors are also options, such as purple or orange, but green and blue are the most positive of the colors.

USE A SLASH RATHER THAN
AN X TO MARK A WRONG ANSWER

Again, for the same reasons one should not use red ink, one should limit the use of an X when evaluating a student's work. In our society, the X is a negative symbol. A slash (/) through the question number does not give the same strong representation as does the X.

Rather than an X or a slash, another possibility is to mark the correct answers with a checkmark and not mark the incorrect ones (although this does tend to clutter up the paper).

INDICATE THE NUMBER
OF CORRECT ANSWERS INSTEAD
OF SUBTRACTING THE NUMBER WRONG

Marking the number correct on the top of the paper accentuates the positive. This can have the same psychological effect as the difference between red and green ink. For example, although the score is poor, "2/20" looks better than "–18."

Teacher Tool

In addition to the self-esteem issue, there are also important cultural concerns with the color red. In some cultures, such as Korean culture, a person's name written in red is a sign of death. Imagine the shock some Korean parents experience when they receive a paper with a personal note to the child written in red!

CONCLUDING THOUGHTS

Self-esteem is affected by many things that the teacher does, on purpose and inadvertently. This is especially the case with marking student papers. Marking papers with green or blue ink instead of red, using a slash instead of an X through incorrect answers, and marking the total number right instead of subtracting the total number wrong are all positive ways to mark papers.

> A teacher has a greater impact on students through less obvious actions that directly affect the students' self-esteem.

FOR FURTHER READING ON THIS SUBJECT

Kottler, J. A., & Kottler, E. (2006). *Counseling skills for teachers* (2nd ed.). Thousand Oaks, CA: Corwin.

Lawrence, D. (2006). *Enhancing self-esteem in the classroom* (3rd ed.). West Yorkshire, England: Paul Chapman.

Plummer, D. M. (2007). *Helping children to build self-esteem: A photocopiable activities book* (2nd ed.). Philadelphia: Jessica Kingsley.

12

A Beginner's Guide to Figuring Grades

It was 11 p.m. and Aliya was still working on her grades. She had been working on them since she got home from school. The numbers didn't make sense—fifteen points for one quiz, twenty-five for another, especially when the quizzes were supposed to be of equal value. She knew the basic level of each of her students, but sometimes the grades seemed to be much lower than expected, especially when a student failed one or two tests but did well on others. How could she improve her grading system?

Grade Levels

3–12

Timeline

All year, especially the week before the first grade report to parents is due

The Issue

What is the easiest, most efficient, and fairest way to determine my students' grades?

THE IDEA

A new teacher at my school was failing an unusual number of middle school students. These weren't "bad" kids—in fact, her class was the only class in which these students received a low grade. The teacher, the counselors, and the administrators were baffled.

When I sat with her to discuss the problem, she showed me a typical student's test scores: 25, 80, 40, 95, and 90. Each number was a percentage of 100, and each test was worth an equal number of points. She averaged these scores to determine a final grade.

Now even though this student had received two As, one B, and two Fs, the final grade given by the teacher was 66 percent, a D. The student and her parents could not understand how this was possible.

How to figure out your grades is one of the basic required teacher skills that is not usually taught in teacher-education programs. Unfortunately, new teachers are expected to pick this up on their own, even though it is an area scrutinized by administrators, counselors, parents, and especially students. More important, it is also an area that invariably results in tremendous amounts of stress for the new teacher.

There is no standard grading system. Each teacher, each curriculum, and each school has particular characteristics that influence how grading should be conducted. The following are basic tips new teachers can use as guides when beginning to develop a personal grading system:

- Use a calculator.
- Use a percentage system based on 100.
- Give all failing grades a score of 50 in your grade book.
- Convert letter grades to their numerical equivalents.
- Establish a final numerical grading formula.
- Be prepared to justify your decisions.

USE A CALCULATOR

This may sound overly simplistic, but a calculator makes your grading much more objective, defendable, and significantly easier to manipulate. Although there are computer grade-book programs, I do not recommend them unless you have an absolute, nonvarying standard of grading. Yes, computerized programs are much easier and do most of the work for you; however, they run on simple equations, with little variation and with limited teacher input or judgment variables possible.

The computerized grade program also limits flexibility and accessibility. For example, I have at times had a student that did poorly on the first few assignments and then turned himself around and earned As and Bs the rest of the semester. With my handwritten grade book, I had the flexibility to simply ignore those early poor scores, without having to reprogram the system.

As far as accessibility, I know many of my fellow teachers that cannot access their grades immediately if a student or parent asks them a question on the spot. They often have to go to their computer, turn it on, and bring up the records. This waiting time can be very frustrating and negative in the eyes of a parent. On the other hand, when faced with a similar situation, I simply walk to my desk and open up my grade book for instant information.

USE A PERCENTAGE SYSTEM BASED ON 100

One of the biggest problems in the roll books of new teachers are column after column of points, which have no immediate meaning and have to be added, weighed, and analyzed in order to be understood. There is an easy solution to making the roll book easy to use and understand. Always convert all grades and numbers to a system of 100. It will not only make it significantly quicker to figure out overall grades, but it will simplify explanations to parents and administrators if they can see the grades in terms of percentages. A score of 85% informs the parent of their child's work quality more clearly than does a score of 17 out of 20 points. Differences between the importance of graded areas (such as quizzes, tests, homework, projects) can then be weighted in the final grade. For example, quizzes may be worth 25%; tests, 50%; homework, 10%; and projects, 15%.

> Fair assessment is the ultimate goal of grading.

Applying a Percentage System Based on 100

- A quiz is worth 30 points.
- The student earned 27 points.
- The score 27/30 gives a percentage of 90 (100 × 27/30 = 90).
- You would write a score of 90 in your roll book instead of a score of 27.

GIVE ALL FAILING GRADES
A SCORE OF 50 IN YOUR GRADE BOOK

This is a critical area where the middle school teacher I spoke of did not take into account that by averaging in any failing mark at its point value, she was unfairly weighting the mark in the overall grade. For instance, if a student takes two tests, scores 0 (an F) on one and 100 (an A+) on the other, it would be logical that an A and an F average out to a C. However, by using just numerical values, the student's average on these two tests is a 50, which usually translates into an F. This is obviously not a fair assessment of that student's work, and fair assessment is the ultimate goal of grading.

Let's review the example that began this chapter:

The student received scores of 25, 80, 40, 95, and 90.

The teacher averaged the scores to come up with 66 percent, a D.

For averaging purposes, however, the student's failing grades should be converted to 50. Her scores would then be 50, 80, 50, 95, and 90 (the failing scores of 25 and 40 would still be marked on the tests, and discussed in parent conferences).

The average percentages for these scores would be 73 percent, a C, which is an improved and a more valid representation of her work.

CONVERT LETTER GRADES
TO THEIR NUMERICAL EQUIVALENTS

It is always easier to average numbers rather than letters; a numerical total is more understandable to other adults, such as parents. Telling parents that their child earned four As, three Bs, and two Cs in spelling for an overall grade of B+ is not as clear as showing the parent scores of 100, 95, 95, 95, 85, 85, 80, 75, and 75, which averages out to 88%, or a B+. There are two ways to work with the numbers: a percentage system (based on 100) and a grade point system (based on 4.0 points, as done in middle school, high school, and college). Both systems work identically, converting letter grades to numerical equivalents. Which you use is simply a matter of preference.

Table 12.1 Converting Letter Grades to Percentages

A + = 100	C + = 78
A = 95	C = 75
A – = 92	C – = 72
B + = 88	D + = 68
B = 85	D = 65
B – = 82	D – = 62
	F = 50

Percentage System

When using a percentage system, you convert all letter grades to specific numerical equivalents, based on a 100-point system. They are then averaged. Table 12.1 includes numerical equivalents for letter grades based on a percentage system.

Grade Point System

In a grade point system, you convert all letter grades to numerical equivalents based on a 4.0 system. You then average them and convert the average back into a letter grade. Table 12.2 contains numerical equivalents for letter grades based on a 4.0 system.

As stated above, after you average the point values, you convert the average into a letter grade. Table 12.2 lists letter-grade equivalents for point ranges in a 4.0 grade point system and for percentage ranges. Decisions about borderline grades are, of course, up to the discretion of the teacher.

If a student received two As, two Bs, one B –, and three Cs, using the 4.0 grade point system, the grade would be

Table 12.2 Converting Letter Grades to Numerical Equivalents Based on a 4.0 System

A + = 4.3	C + = 2.3
A = 4.0	C = 2.0
A – = 3.7	C – = 1.7
B + = 3.3	D + = 1.3
B = 3.0	D = 1.0
B – = 2.7	D – = 0.7
	F = 0.0

$$(2 \times 4) + (2 \times 3) + (1 \times 2.7) + (3 \times 2) = 8 + 6 + 2.7 + 6 = 22.7$$
22.7 (total points) divided by 8 grades
(total number of grades) = 2.8, a low B.

With simple mental calculations and your calculator, this grade takes about fifteen to twenty seconds to figure out, at the most.

ESTABLISH A FINAL NUMERICAL GRADING FORMULA

Before determining the final grades, decide the weight, or importance, you wish to give to each of the grade areas. The following is an example:

Tests: 50%

Quizzes: 25%

Project: 25%

Using these percentages in my example, the following is how I would figure out a typical student's grade:

Tests = 86% = 86 × 2 = 172 (Tests are worth twice as much as the other two areas; therefore, I double the final percentage.)

Quizzes = 79% = 79 × 1 = 79

Project = 92% = 92 × 1 = 92

Total = 172 + 79 + 92 = 343 divided by 4 (4 parts: tests twice, quizzes, project) = 85.75, which I round up to 86, a B.

In Table 12.3, there are five different grade categories. Rarely will you have such a complicated situation, but if you do, the following is an example of how to compute the final grade easily:

Table 12.3   Weighting Grades in Five Categories

Category	Grade Weight	Student's Average Percentage	Score Multiplied by Weight	Point Total
Tests	30 percent	80 percent	80 × 3 parts*	240
Quizzes	30 percent	90 percent	90 × 3 parts	270
Project	20 percent	75 percent	75 × 2 parts	150
Homework	10 percent	92 percent	92 × 1 part	92
Class work	10 percent	75 percent	75 × 1 part	75
Total: 240 + 270 + 150 + 92 + 75 = 827, divided by 10 parts = 82.7, rounded up to 83 = B				

*3 parts of 10 total: always use a scale of 100 to make calculations easier.

Although it may appear involved, the process goes quickly after you get used to it. (A calculator is invaluable, for it makes these calculations easy.) Most important, this process is fair and defendable, the two most important factors in grading, especially for new teachers, as the next section explains.

BE PREPARED TO JUSTIFY YOUR DECISIONS

A new teacher should always role-play as the grades are formulated. For example, assume the role of a parent who is going to question your decisions about his or her child's poor grade. Ask yourself if, based on the evidence in the roll book, you can objectively justify the grade. If you can, if the numbers add up correctly to support the mark, then the grade stands. If you notice a discrepancy, go back and see where the problem lies and correct it.

CONCLUDING THOUGHTS

Determining grades can be simple or time-consuming, depending on how you plan for it. Not being careful when converting letter marks to numerical scores and vice versa can be unfair to the student. For grades to be easy to understand, efficient to calculate, and fair, always use a calculator, incorporate a percentage system (a system based on 100), give failing grades below 50 a score of 50 when you average the scores, convert letter grades to numbers, and be able to justify your decisions and policy.

FOR FURTHER READING ON THIS SUBJECT

Guskey, T. R. (2008). *Practical solutions for serious problems in standards-based grading.* Thousand Oaks, CA: Corwin.

Mierzwik, D. (2005). *Classroom record keeping made simple: Tips for time-strapped teachers.* Thousand Oaks, CA: Corwin.

Wormeli, R. (2006). *Fair isn't always equal: Assessing & grading in the differentiated classroom.* Portland, ME: Stenhouse.

13

Rubrics

Aliya wanted to create a rubric for a special project. With a rubric, the students would know exactly what her expectations were and what the minimum requirements were for a certain grade. However, when the projects were completed, she discovered that many of them, though excellent, did not fit the rubric requirements. She felt boxed in. These were projects she felt deserved an A, but with her new rubric, she could not give them such a high mark.

Grade Levels

K–12

Timeline

All year, but especially before the first major project or report you assign

The Issue

How can I create a rubric that is valid and fair?

THE IDEA

In this age of NCLB standards-based instruction, many schools are now requiring that teachers grade all student work according to a rubric. Rubrics are usually based on either a letter scale of A through F, or a numerical scale of 4 to 1. Some elementary schools have eliminated grades altogether and now evaluate all student work on a 4–1 rubric (with a 3 representing "meets state standards").

All teachers, new and experienced, become nervous when constructing their first rubric. They question whether they are constructing it correctly and whether it will adequately assess their students. These worries are really unnecessary. All teachers use rubrics, even if they are not formally written down. All teachers have standards for what will constitute an A, a B, and so on. When new assignments are given, share your standards with your students. Consequently, these students will have clear expectations for what is required. Always provide concrete examples of what constitutes A work. These are the essential steps of working with rubrics.

It's when you transcribe these rubrics onto paper that problems arise. The following tips will help ensure your rubrics are valid, fair, and useable:

- Make sure the rubric reflects your goals.
- Be only as specific as you need to be.
- Allow for exceptions.

MAKE SURE THE RUBRIC REFLECTS YOUR GOALS

All evaluations should measure whether the students have met your lesson or unit goals. This is also true for rubrics. For example, if your goal is for students to learn X, Y, and Z from the history unit, then the rubric should be based on the students demonstrating knowledge of X, Y, and Z. If your goal is for the students to synthesize material into an original project, your rubric needs to reflect aspects of the synthesis of material and the creativity of the students.

More important, always be sure to provide the students with concrete examples of what constitutes the highest level of the rubric. Students should have clear understanding of what you require before they begin. There are no right or wrong rubrics. Know what you want to teach and use the rubric to determine if it was learned.

BE ONLY AS SPECIFIC AS YOU NEED TO BE

The most common problem with rubrics is that they are too specific. For example, a rubric that is too specific may state "To earn an A, use eight facts in a three-paragraph essay, with no grammatical mistakes and no spelling errors." What happens if a student uses only seven facts?

All teachers use rubrics, even if they are not formally written down. All teachers have standards for what will constitute an A, a B, and so on.

Has one short paragraph? Or misses a punctuation mark? Does this student, who did not meet the exact requirements of the rubric in one aspect, now get a B? How about the student who uses twelve facts in two long, well-written paragraphs?

The more specific you are, the more you are limited. A better rubric might be "For an A, write a well-written two-page essay, incorporating information from the chapter in the essay. Grammar and spelling mistakes must be at a minimum." Be sure to provide some examples of what you consider a "well-written two-page essay."

This is just one example. There are many other possibilities for your rubric, but you can see how this general rubric provides you with enough leeway for exceptions, while evaluating whether the students have met your goals. Above all, be careful that the rubric does not become a checklist, which doesn't enable you to make value judgments. This is a common problem with new teachers creating rubrics for the first time.

ALLOW FOR EXCEPTIONS

This concept, more than anything else, relates to the fairness of your rubric. Being fair is primary for all grading and interaction with your students. Nothing will cause you to lose your students' respect more quickly than when they feel you are not fair, especially in your grading practices.

If student work does not fit the rubric but deserves a certain grade in your mind, give it that grade. Whenever you present the rubric to the class, always remind the students that you reserve the right to alter a grade, if deserved. If this happens, sit down with the student and objectively justify your decision. In this fashion, students see that you are being fair.

Other teachers on staff usually have examples of rubrics to share. Look through them and see what you like and don't like, then construct your own. Table 13.1 shows examples of rubrics created by an eighth-grade English teacher.

Teacher Tool

If you do not want to create an entire rubric from scratch, there are many online sites where you can either make or take rubrics for your various classes. Some excellent free sites are Rubistar (rubistar.4teachers.org/index.php), Rubrics 4 Teachers (www.rubrics4teachers.com), and Rubrics and Evaluation Resources (www.ncsu.edu/midlink/ho.html).

CONCLUDING THOUGHTS

Rubrics are being used increasingly in schools around the country. However, they can be limiting and produce unfair grading. When constructing rubrics, make sure that the rubrics reflect your goals, that they are only as specific as you need, and that they allow for exceptions.

Table 13.1   Examples of Rubrics

Rubric for Major Composition	
4 Advanced	• Clearly states a thesis/point of view • Contains three paragraphs: introduction, body, and conclusion • Each paragraph has a topic sentence that is well-supported with evidence • Ideas are well organized for the reader • Appropriate use of conventions
3 Proficient	• Clearly states a thesis/point of view • Contains three paragraphs: introduction, body, and conclusion • Each paragraph has a topic sentence with some support with evidence • Ideas are mostly well organized for the reader • Mostly appropriate use of conventions
2 Partially Proficient	• States a thesis/point of view, but it is unclear • Contains three paragraphs: introduction, body, and conclusion • Ideas are somewhat confusing to the reader • Attempted appropriate use of conventions
1 Not Proficient	• No thesis/point of view • Does not use three paragraph format • Ideas are too confusing to be followed by the reader • No attempt at appropriate use of conventions
Rubric for a Sentence Poster	
4 Advanced	• Space is effectively and attractively used • All work is neat and complete • Required sentence structure is used with *no* errors: 3 compound, 2 complex sentences • All necessary information is used in the text
3 Proficient	• Space is mostly effectively and attractively used • Most work is neat and complete • Required sentence structure is used with few errors • Most necessary information is used in the text
2 Partially Proficient	• Some attempt is made to use space effectively and attractively • Work is not neat and is incomplete • Some required sentence structure is missing • Some necessary information is missing from the text
1 Not Proficient	• Little attempt is made to use space effectively or attractively • Work is not neat and is incomplete • Little or no required sentence structure is correctly used • Significant necessary information is missing

Source: Created by Kathie Marshall, Pacoima Middle School, Los Angeles, California. Reprinted with permission.

FOR FURTHER READING ON THIS SUBJECT

Burke, K. (2006). *From standards to rubrics in six steps: Tools for assessing student learning, K–8.* Thousand Oaks, CA: Corwin.

Lazear, D. (1998). *The rubrics way: Using MI to assess understanding.* Chicago: Zephyr Press.

Stevens, D. D., & Levi, A. J. (2004). *Introduction to rubrics: An assessment tool to save grading time, convey effective feedback and promote student learning.* Sterling, VA: Stylus.

14

Grading for Classroom Participation

Aliya was working on her grades and was uncomfortable giving a grade for class participation, although it seemed to be a standard grading area within her school. In her class, there were two students who always participated, always had their hands up, and almost always had an incorrect answer. At the same time, she had a student who never raised her hand but would always know the answer when called upon and did well on all the assignments she completed. How could she justify giving these three students classroom participation grades?

Grade Levels

3–12

Timeline

All year, but especially the week when you figure out final grades

The Issue

Should I grade classroom participation?

THE IDEA

Student participation in class is a direct result of leadership personality traits. (For a report of the research on the leadership personality as it relates to classroom performance, see Mandel, 1991.) Students with strong leadership personalities enjoy raising their hands even if they are consistently incorrect. Those with weak leadership personalities are extremely reluctant to raise their hands, even if they know the correct answer. This does not mean that these students are less on-task than those who continually raise their hands. Nor is the contrary true. Therefore, if you give points for classroom participation, in actuality, you are rewarding those with a strong leadership personality style and punishing those with a weak one.

Leadership is a personality trait. We are all on a leadership continuum. On one end, there are those who thoroughly enjoy and seek out leadership roles. On the other end, there are those who actively avoid a participatory status when compelled to work with a group.

Teacher Tool

Think about your group work experiences in college or your association with school committees. Did you take over the group's leadership? Did you take an active and participatory role? Did you sit back and take a minimal role in the group discussion? It was your personal leadership style that served as the single greatest determining factor of the degree of your group participation.

During a study of cooperative learning in the classroom, small-group work was videotaped during four different extensive cooperative learning units (Mandel, 2003). The videotapes were then analyzed and the types of leadership shown within the various small working groups explored. Each student was classified as fulfilling one of four leadership roles:

- *Task leadership:* This student is concerned with the process—keeping others on task, getting supplies, and so forth.
- *Intellectual leadership:* This student offers new ideas to the group (versus simply answering someone's question with a research result).
- *Social and emotional leadership:* This student gives praise or encouragement to members of the group.
- *Coercive leadership:* This student gives negative feedback or creates off-topic humor to disrupt the process, even momentarily.

At the same time, based on their group participation, the students were also classified as one of the following:

- *Leaders:* These students control all facets of the group and initiate virtually all of the dialogue among members. They may show task leadership one day and intellectual or social leadership the next. The leadership roles change depending on what other leader happens to be in their group on that particular day.

- *Followers:* These students answer questions and participate, but usually only at the instigation of one of the leaders.
- *Nonparticipants:* These students never offer information unless asked; they never volunteer for anything. However, they routinely do whatever task is assigned to them.

Amazingly, it was discovered that the only students who ever took significant leadership roles within the group were those students who had been categorized as leaders. Followers sometimes showed some leadership characteristics, but always at the instigation of the leaders. Nonparticipants never took any leadership roles; they answered questions when asked, using the shortest possible answers, and they quietly did their work without any interaction with others.

WHAT THIS MEANS FOR CLASSROOM PARTICIPATION GRADING

Applying leadership concepts to the classroom is quite easy and enlightening. Students with strong leadership personality traits will always raise their hands. It is irrelevant whether they know they have the correct answer. Their desire to lead is stronger than any negative reinforcement you may give for incorrect answers. At the same time, nonparticipants—those you know have the correct answer—will never raise their hands. It is simply too uncomfortable for them. Therefore, you are actually grading students on their leadership personality trait, not whether they are attentive to your lessons, when you grade for classroom participation.

CONCLUDING THOUGHTS

When you grade for classroom participation, you are actually grading the students' leadership personality styles. Often those who consistently raise their hands do not know the material, while those who do not raise their hands may know it quite well.

> You are actually grading students on their leadership personality trait, not whether they are attentive to your lessons, when you grade for classroom participation.

FOR FURTHER READING ON THIS SUBJECT

Bender, Y. (2004). *The power of positive teaching: 35 successful strategies for active and enthusiastic classroom participation.* White River Junction, VT: Nomad Press.

Burchard, B. (2008). *The student leadership guide* (4th ed.). Garden City, NY: Morgan James.

Mandel, S. (2003). *Cooperative work groups: Preparing students for the real world.* Thousand Oaks, CA: Corwin.

15

A Student Self-Esteem Check

Aliya was concerned about her students' self-esteem. It all started when one of her "problem" students accused her of always picking on him and letting others get away with the same behavior. Aliya had always tried to be fair, but she began to question whether this student was correct in his assessment of her.

Grade Levels

K–12

Timeline

All year, but especially around the third or fourth month, after you are comfortable with your students and curriculum

The Issue

How can I verify that self-esteem is being fostered in my classroom environment?

THE IDEA

There is such a thing as a hidden curriculum, which has a tremendous impact on your classroom, especially in the realm of the self-esteem of your students. As you know, students' self-esteem has a tremendous effect on their academic achievement and their behavior. The hidden curriculum consists of things a teacher does that the students react to, actions that reveal the teacher's attitudes and feelings, of which the teacher is often unaware.

This chapter is intended for personal reflection and analysis, a self-check on how you are doing. Too often during the first year, teachers are so involved in getting the curriculum right, correctly following all school procedures, and concentrating on the students' academics that much of the material included in this chapter gets lost in the shuffle, albeit unintentionally. As you go through this section, if you find areas of concern, refer to the appropriate chapters of this book for suggestions on how to alleviate the problem.

There are a number of areas in which you can conduct a self-assessment to determine the level of student self-esteem in your classroom:

- Interactions with students
- The classroom environment
- Student profiles

Take time to reflect on the following issues. This exercise is meant to be a private self-analysis and should serve as a means of examining the self-esteem level being fostered in your classroom. After completing all of the following steps, reflect on the type of classroom you described and whether there is anything you wish to change or modify in the future.

INTERACTIONS WITH STUDENTS

Choose three students who recently required some form of discipline. In each case, comment on the following:

What type of discipline did you use? Determine whether the student committed a

- minor offense, requiring only a reprimand;
- medium offense, requiring a reprimand and a privilege taken away or a punishment given;
- somewhat major offense, requiring a harsher punishment (such as a citation, detention, referral); or
- major offense, requiring the parent and administrator, counselor, or dean to become directly involved.

(Note that the terms *minor*, *medium*, and *major* are subjective and vary from school to school. Meet with the administrator in charge of discipline or your department head and ask for examples.)

How did you conduct your response to the student? Did you talk to the student

- privately, with no other students present?
- privately, with other students present in the class but none within hearing distance?

- semi-privately, with other students present in the class and a few close enough to hear if they listened?
- publicly, where all students in the class could hear the exchange?

Recall and summarize the student's behavior and work habits immediately after the exchange.

Recall and summarize the student's behavior and work habits over the next hour or two after the exchange, or throughout the remainder of the class period in secondary school.

The hidden curriculum consists of things a teacher does that the students react to, actions that reveal the teacher's attitudes and feelings, of which the teacher is often unaware.

Recall and summarize the student's behavior and work habits the next school day.

Do you notice any correlation between the way you interacted with the student and that student's subsequent behaviors?

THE CLASSROOM ENVIRONMENT

Survey the classroom, concentrating on the student work displayed. Count and record how much of the work is from

- academically above-average students,
- academically average students, or
- academically below-average students.

Keeping in mind the above three categories, examine where the work is displayed:

- Location in the classroom (front wall, back wall, and so forth)
- Position in the display (center, outer edge, and so forth)

STUDENT PROFILES

Individual student profiles provide a great deal of information about the self-esteem of your students. Randomly select three to five students from your roll book. For example, pick every fifth student. You can also select students who have had behavioral or academic problems. In either situation, write a short student profile, answering each of the following questions:

What is the student's appearance and attitude when he or she initially enters your class?

- Describe mood, based on facial expressions and mannerisms (such as depressed, as seen in a lethargic walk, or happy, as evident in a grin).
- Describe the student's physical appearance, comparing it to the appearance of other students in the class.

With whom does this student socialize?

- Take into account the type of students, such as academically oriented, sports- or club-oriented, those with discipline problems, or those who are ethnically similar.
- Observe the student from your desk during a work period, when student interactions are permitted. With whom does the student interact? Tally the number of different students interacted with during this exercise.

Describe the student's reactions after being given an assignment with a poor grade and after receiving a good grade.

Describe the types of parent contact you have had (such as personal, verbal, or written).

- Recall how the parents have acted.
- Assume the student's place and imagine the type of parent interaction she has concerning school matters.

This has been an exercise in reflection. These questions and activities are meant to bring information to your mind about your classroom. The next two steps are yours:

- What do my observations mean?
- Based on my observations, what can I do to make my classroom better?

These are questions only you can analyze. Turn to what you have learned in this book, to what you have learned in your education classes, and to your fellow staff members for help finding answers.

MODELING RESPECT

More than anything else, the students see you model respect. The material in this chapter up to now concerned your relationships with students. How you relate to adults is also keenly observed by your students. For example, ask yourself about your behavior whenever there are any students present:

- Do you talk with respect to all other teachers, administrators, and parents?
- When other adults display disrespect towards you, do you answer them similarly, or maintain your level of respect?
- When you mention other teachers, administrators, or parents to your students, do you "editorialize" through words, facial expression, or body language?

These are simply additional areas to examine closely in your quest to raise your student's self-esteem and respect.

CONCLUDING THOUGHTS

Your every action can affect your students in some fashion, especially in the realm of self-esteem. Therefore, you should regularly do a self-esteem check of your classroom to see how things are going by examining your interactions with students and your classroom environment and by conducting student profiles.

FOR FURTHER READING ON THIS SUBJECT

Lawrence, D. (2006). *Enhancing self-esteem in the classroom* (3rd ed.). West Yorkshire, England: Paul Chapman.

Plummer, D. M. (2007). *Helping children to build self-esteem: A photocopiable activities book* (2nd ed.). Philadelphia: Jessica Kingsley.

Podesta, C. (2001). *Self-esteem and the 6-second secret*. Thousand Oaks, CA: Corwin.

PART IV

Parents

✓ **Parent Involvement**

How can I get parents positively involved in my educational program?

✓ **Parent-Teacher Conferences**

How can I conduct a successful parent-teacher conference?

16

Parent Involvement

Aliya was concerned about her students' parents. She wanted to get them involved in their children's education, but at the same time, she wished to avoid complaints or directions for how she should run her classroom. Aliya knew that the more parents "bought into" her classroom program, the more supportive they would be, and the more successful their children. How could she accomplish this task?*

Grade Levels

K–8

Timeline

All year, but especially during the first month of school

The Issue

How can I get parents involved positively in my educational program?

THE IDEA

The more that parents feel involved in your classroom program, the more supportive they will be of your classroom curriculum, and the more they will

---

*Basic ideas in this chapter were submitted by Debora Mcdonnell, Jefferson Elementary School, Norman, Oklahoma.

"buy in" to what you are trying to do. Initiate programs that will help get the parents involved, and ultimately they will become supportive of you in the classroom. As you review the ideas in this chapter, choose what will work with your particular teaching assignment and students. There are numerous ways to involve parents:

- Make start-up phone calls.
- Initiate a calling web.
- Create and send out a questionnaire.
- Create a suggestion box.
- Create a Thursday folder for each student.
- Create a monthly calendar.
- Establish office hours.
- Create a weekly newsletter.
- Follow up with parents as necessary by telephone.
- Create a bulletin board that features particular students and their families and cultures.
- Put together a parent bookshelf.

START-UP CALLS

The first thing you should do is spend some time the first week or two of school calling each parent to introduce yourself. You should be able to get a list of names and phone numbers from the office responsible for student assignments. Nowadays, it may be as simple as printing a computer list.

Remember that the more parents understand what you are trying to do, the more they will support your program, and the fewer problems or misunderstandings will result throughout the year.

When you speak with parents, emphasize the importance of parent involvement from the start and that you would like open lines of communication. If you have a Back to School Night at your school, remind them of the date. If not, schedule a meeting for a time when the most parents can attend to learn about your classroom curriculum and policies.

CALLING WEB

Early in the year, establish a calling web. A calling web is used to inform and remind parents about special programs or requests in the classroom (such as field trips or materials needed for an art project) or in the school (such as an open house or canned goods needed for a food drive). Each parent will be responsible for telephoning two or three other parents to notify them of special events or news.

When creating a calling web, be sure to match non-English-speaking parents to other parents who speak the same language. This will also address communication issues for those who are not fluent in reading English. If no one else speaks a parent's language, use a school translator to communicate with that parent or, at last resort, seek the help of responsible students who speak the language. This will ensure that your non-English-speaking parents will feel included and involved in your classroom program.

BEGINNING OF THE YEAR QUESTIONNAIRE

You can collect an immense amount of helpful information by sending parents a questionnaire early in the year. Include questions that elicit information about both the child and the parents. Not only will you find out general information about a child and parents, but this also gives the parents an opportunity to share certain things about their child that you need to know, such as whether their child has ADD/ADHD, or whether there is a crisis in the child's life, such as a pending divorce or a terminally ill grandparent. These things will directly affect the child's academic and behavior performance in your classroom, and having knowledge of it will assist you in helping and understanding the child before or when problems arise. For example, your questionnaire could include questions such as the following:

- What are your child's interests?
- What do you think is important for your child to learn this year?
- Do you have insights about your child you would like to share?
- Would you like to be involved in the classroom? How?
- Does your child take any medication that might affect his class performance?
- Is anything happening in your child's home life that might affect her class performance?

Initiate programs that will help get the parents involved, and ultimately they will become supportive of you in the classroom.

SUGGESTION BOX

A helpful tool for year-round communication is a suggestion box, mounted near the classroom door, for student and parent suggestions. Let it be known that anonymous suggestions are welcome. Discuss this box at Back to School Night if your school has one. Tell parents and students that you will review all suggestions, but that school district and state policies will have the final say as to whether the suggestions will be incorporated into the curriculum. Always thank the parents and students for their ideas, explaining why you chose to use or not use them.

THURSDAY FOLDER NOTES

A great means of establishing good communication is to send home a folder on Thursday to be returned on Monday, containing student work and school communication items. Include a section that is permanently attached for handwritten comments and communication between parent and teacher. This establishes a written record of your communication with the home. By sending it home on Thursday, you give the parent an opportunity to respond over the weekend. Returning the folder on Monday is considered homework.

MONTHLY CALENDAR

At the beginning of each month, send home a calendar highlighting times when parent participation on a school or class level would be appreciated. In an elementary school, include times in your daily schedule when parents are welcome to visit, such as during a study hall or reading time. Invite parents to lunch, recess, library times, lab time, and special activities. If possible, schedule at least one event a month that will occur in the evening (for working parents). These can easily be curricular events. For example, have an authors' tea where students share works they have published. Set up an art museum for parents to visit. Have parents inform you if they have an idea for an event. A calendar gives parents an opportunity to plan in advance, in addition to providing a variety of options for participation from which to choose. (Be sure to check with your administrator regarding policies on parent visitation and after-hours use of the classroom, and notify parents of any policies that affect them.)

OFFICE HOURS

One easy way to establish parent contact opportunities is to have one evening or afternoon a week listed on the classroom calendar when you will be available, either in the classroom or by telephone, to speak with parents. Periodically change the time to ensure availability to all parents. Many parents now correspond with teachers by e-mail. E-mail allows a teacher to respond any time in the evening, without getting into a long discussion with a parent. If further conversation is needed, you can set up a follow-up phone call.

Most problems between the teacher and parent are a result of miscommunication or lack of communication. Many communication problems can be alleviated before they even start by establishing formal opportunities for contact.

If you have room parents, change the parent with each new grade period. This will involve more parents, and the workload won't fall on only one or two persons. However, this should be very clearly communicated in September, or feelings may be hurt because the parents may feel they are being "fired" from the job.

WEEKLY NEWSLETTERS

Another great communication tool is a newsletter, which can be put in the Thursday folders. Always include a translation in the home language if a non-English-speaking parent is monolingual. Check with your school's office manager to find out how your school handles translations, or use the Web site Alta Vista Babel Fish Translation (www.babelfish.altavista.com) to translate your notices (see Mandel, 2007, pp. 46–47, for an explanation on how this site operates). Use the newsletter to thank parents, acknowledge their assistance, and inform them of any new programs. You can also provide information about curricular subjects or projects to be completed the following week.

TELEPHONE CALLS

When parents don't respond to written communication, periodically telephone them to request their participation and their input. (If they do not speak English, enlist the help of their web caller or a school staff member who speaks their language.) Do not let these calls become phone conferences. If a parent wants you to go into detail about his or her child, set up an appointment either in person or at another time on the phone when the only topic will concern the child's progress.

BULLETIN BOARD FEATURE

In the elementary grades, establish a specific bulletin board to highlight individual students, their families, and their cultural heritage on a one- or two-week rotating basis. Encourage the parents to help the student plan the board. Send each family a note explaining it, with suggestions and a sign-up schedule. Be prepared to assist students who have noninvolved parents.

PARENT BOOKSHELF

Most problems between the teacher and parent are a result of miscommunication or lack of communication.

Parent education is an important aspect of parent involvement. Parents often want to learn more about both parenting and their child's curriculum. It's helpful to have books, even if only a few, available to parents on a specifically designated shelf in your room.

> ### Teacher Tool
>
> One of the best public relations tools you can use with parents is to make sure you periodically call each student and parent with good news. Some of your students have probably never received a good news call from their teacher.

Be sure to include books on parenting, homework and study skills, and curricular subjects your students will study in both English and the language the parents read, as well as anything else you feel is useful, such as the books listed at the end of this chapter.

CONCLUDING THOUGHTS

There are a number of things that you can do to positively involve parents in your classroom. These include making start-up calls to the parents; establishing a telephone calling web; sending home a questionnaire; setting up a suggestion box; creating Thursday folders; creating monthly calendars; establishing office hours; rotating your room parents; writing a weekly newsletter; making regular telephone calls to the home; developing a section of the bulletin board to feature families; and establishing a parent bookshelf.

FOR FURTHER READING ON THIS SUBJECT

Boult, B. (2006). *176 ways to involve parents: Practical strategies for partnering with families* (2nd ed.). Thousand Oaks, CA: Corwin.

Mandel, S. (2007). *The parent-teacher partnership: How to work together for student achievement.* Chicago: Zephyr Press.

Wright, K. (2002). *Building school and community partnerships through parent involvement* (2nd ed.). Upper Saddle River, NJ: Prentice Hall.

17

Parent-Teacher Conferences

It was parent-teacher conference time, and Aliya was worried. She had heard horror stories from teachers about certain parents. As a new teacher, she feared that the parents would not be satisfied with what she said and would subsequently complain to the principal. At the same time, she had so much she wanted to share with certain parents. How could she make her first experience with a parent-teacher conference successful?

Grade Levels

K–12

Timeline

All year, but especially when the school schedules formal parent conferences

The Issue

How can I conduct a successful parent-teacher conference?

THE IDEA

Parent-teacher conferences are an excellent public relations tool. Too often, parents are dissatisfied with a teacher because they hear only one side of the story at home—their child's side. A face-to-face meeting provides the opportunity to put things into perspective, to explain your decisions, grades you have given, and your basic educational philosophy. It also allows the parents to share their concerns and to ask questions. The parent will often provide you with home-life information that will give you additional insights about the student.

To ensure a positive and successful parent-teacher conference, adhere to the following basic concepts.

- *Remember: The parent is an ally, not an enemy.* Parents who attend conferences want their child to succeed. They are concerned enough to come to school and meet with you. Treat them as an ally and partner with whom to work cooperatively in resolving problems. When you have negative information to share, use an introductory statement such as: "We have a problem" versus "Your child . . ." The latter immediately places parents on the defensive and jeopardizes their cooperation.
- *Create a nonthreatening seating arrangement.* Too often parents are seated across a table from the teacher. This is a power arrangement that places the parent in the position of "student." A more equitable arrangement is suggested as follows:
  o If the student *is not* at the conference, sit next to the parent, giving the feeling that you two are partners.
  o If the student *is* at the conference, sit in a circle, giving the feeling that everyone is equally participating.
- *Always begin with a positive comment.* Though for some students this may be difficult, it is essential for you to establish a positive tone. For the parents of problem students, an immediate positive comment from the teacher "shocks" them in a good way, for they have rarely heard positive statements regarding their child during previous parent-teacher conferences.
- *Insist on the presence of the student.* This is my number-one rule for parent conferences. In fact, I normally refuse to hold the conference if the student is not present. The student's presence prevents miscommunication over what is said at the conference and during the subsequent discussion that occurs at home. In addition, it places the entire focus on the child. The student should be required to respond to what the teacher reports, which results in the student's taking ownership of any problems and their solutions. It becomes much more difficult for students to dispute what you say while sitting there with you and their parents.
- *Use positive statements for personal qualities, negative statements only for student behavior.* As much as parents may agree with your assessments, the student is still their child. Negative personal statements, even if true, may make a parent defensive. An example of a positive personal-quality statement: "He's so conscientious with his work! What a good student." An example of a negative behavior statement: "His lack of attention causes him to miss material that appears on the test." In this statement, the negativity is focused on the behavior exhibited, not on the personality of the student.

- *Be objective.* Use facts when reporting on a student's academic progress, not adjectives or opinions. It is much more difficult for a parent to disagree when you have facts at your disposal. The basic rule of thumb is, if you can't validate it, don't say it. An example would be "She has failed three of four tests this month" rather than "She does not care about her work."
- *Explain the student's progress in easy-to-understand numerical values.* As is explained in Chapter 12, "A Beginner's Guide to Figuring Grades," percentages are easier to understand than raw number scores. Don't say, "He's flunked most of his quizzes," or "He's flunked nine of fifteen quizzes." Instead say, "He's failed 60% of his quizzes." Don't say, "She has 450 points out of 600 to date." That type of statistic is difficult for parents to grasp. Rather say, "She has earned 75% of the possible number of points to date."

> The student should be required to respond to what the teacher reports, which results in the student's taking ownership of any problems and their solutions.

- *Do not say anything that you cannot defend.* Role-play in your mind a scenario in which every parent who hears a negative statement from you complains and you are called on each issue. Ask yourself, "Can I defend my position with the roll book?" If you have objective proof, then go ahead and make the statement. If not, reevaluate your position.
- *Do not take any abuse.* You are a professional and should insist upon being treated with respect. Warn any parents who raise their voices or use inappropriate language that you won't tolerate it. If it happens again with a parent, terminate the conference, whether in person or on the telephone. For example, you can say, "Thank you, Mr./Mrs. _____, for coming to this conference. I am afraid that we will need to continue this discussion at another time when you are more calm." Afterward, immediate write up the incident, including what you said, what the parent said, and where and when it happened. Be accurate and specific. Do not write, "She used obscene language." Quote the parent directly. Give the documentation to your administrator and keep a copy for your files.
- *If they cannot make one of your times, make one of theirs.* Some parents are unable to attend a daytime conference. It is to *your* benefit to meet them, especially if it means that you have one more supportive parent in your corner. If you feel a conference will help the student succeed, do whatever is necessary to make the essential parent connection.
- *Parent conferences begin on the school's opening day, not at formal parent-teacher conference time.* One big issue parents often have with teachers is finding out there is a problem at the formally scheduled parent-teacher conference time, even though the problem existed for weeks prior. Regular teacher contact with parents throughout the year prevents this situation. A parent should always have a good idea of what a report card will say before receiving it.

CONCLUDING THOUGHTS

Parent conferences are a great opportunity to explain your program and gain support from parents. Always begin with a comfortable, nonthreatening seating arrangement and a positive comment, then provide details about their child's level of achievement. Remember to treat the parents as allies, not enemies.

Always insist on the student being present and use positive statements when commenting on the student's personal qualities, restricting negative statements to behaviors. Always be objective and explain a student's progress into easy-to-understand numerical values. Do not say anything that you cannot defend. Always be the professional! Do not take any abuse. Be flexible in scheduling so you can meet with every parent, and remember: Parent conferences are not restricted to one or two days per academic year.

FOR FURTHER READING ON THIS SUBJECT

Mandel, S. (2007). *The parent-teacher partnership: How to work together for student achievement.* Chicago: Zephyr Press.

Rudney, G. L. (2005). *Every teacher's guide to working with parents.* Thousand Oaks, CA: Corwin.

Tingley, S. C. (2006). *How to handle difficult parents: A teacher's survival guide.* Fort Collins, CO: Cottonwood Press.

PART V

Students Who Have Special Needs

✓ **Modifying the Classroom Curriculum for Students With Special Needs**

How can I modify my classroom curriculum for students with special needs?

✓ **Full-Inclusion Mainstreaming**

What can I, as a non-special education teacher, do to adapt the program for a full-inclusion mainstreamed student?

✓ **Students With ADD/ADHD and Classroom Management**

How can I modify my classroom procedures for students with severe behavioral problems?

✓ **Preparing for a Special Education Class**

What do I need to do to organize a special education class?

18

Modifying the Classroom Curriculum for Students With Special Needs

A liya was assigned two students who had special needs. Both were in special pullout programs for one of their academic subjects and remained in the classroom for all the others; however, their learning disabilities affected their performance in all subject areas, not just in the one for which they were pulled out for extra assistance. What modifications could Aliya apply to meet the needs of these students without disrupting her classroom curriculum?*

Grade Levels

K–12

Timeline

All year, but especially the first month with your students

The Issue

How can I modify my classroom curriculum for students with special needs?

---

*Basic ideas in this chapter were contributed by Jan Demontigny, Farm Hill Elementary School, Middletown, Connecticut.

THE IDEA

After you have read the students' individualized education plans (IEPs) and located any required modifications, consider other simple modifications you can use to assist students with disabilities in the general classroom. Many are not time consuming and can make a major difference in these students' learning. In the following list are a number of ideas that can be adopted in any classroom.

- *When you assign independent work, give it to the student in small segments.* This does not mean you discard some of the normal workload. For example, you could fold a test or a worksheet in half, then ask the student to do the first half and come up for further directions when finished. This prevents the student from feeling rushed or overwhelmed with the amount of work given.
- *Provide either additional time (such as an extra weekend for a weekday assignment) or reduce the length or scope of an assignment.* This is especially important if the assignment covers an area in which the student has difficulty. For example, if the student is pulled out for reading, then a reading assignment in history may have to be reduced, depending on the student's overall disability. However, when giving additional time, be careful how this is done. Students with special needs are very sensitive to appearing singled out or embarrassed, so figure out how to subtly provide any time modifications.
- *In your lesson plans, note the objective you want the particular student to master.* The objectives for the student with special needs do not need to be the same as those for the rest of the class. Review the student's IEP to learn what objectives the student is required to meet. For example, the class might be expected to write a paragraph about a topic, and a student with a severe learning disability in your class might be expected to write three facts. A student with fine motor problems could write some of these facts, and you or a peer helper could take dictation on the rest.
- *Present information in a variety of modalities, particularly visually and orally.* Every student has his or her own unique learning style. Incorporating all modalities will help all the students in your class. Regularly incorporate the use of an overhead projector, posters, pocket charts, and the chalkboard into your lessons. Whenever possible, tie in a hands-on component as well.
- *If a student cannot do what everyone else in the class is doing, modify the work.* No student should be set up for failure. Modifications can avoid this problem, and they are easily accomplished. For example, if the class is working on a subtraction with regrouping worksheet, cut the problems out and use the rest of the original worksheet as a frame for a modified worksheet. Create some problems appropriate to the student's level (for example, double-digit subtraction with no regrouping, or subtraction facts to 18) and paste them onto the modified original. After you photocopy it, the student has a worksheet

that looks like everyone else's, but that enables the student to do work at his or her own level. Be sure to keep a copy for use in future years.

- *Have a wide variety of multilevel reading material in your classroom.* All students should be able to read something in your classroom—no one should be left out.

Teacher Tool

Have students do simple physical exercises before writing. This can involve such things as teaching the students with special needs to push the palms of their hands together, push down hard on a desktop, and squeeze and relax their fists.

- *Use story maps and other graphic organizers to assist students with writing tasks.* Outlines in particular help students with learning disabilities to search for meaning when they read. Make up a chapter outline and give it to all students. It teaches them to focus on the important points in a chapter. To learn how to teach mapping and other graphic organizer skills, see *Mapping Inner Space,* by Nancy Margulies with Nusa Maal (2002).
- *Use color-coded index cards in a file box to keep track of your students' objectives and modifications.* The students' names should not be on these cards. By color coding, you have the information handy without violating confidentiality. If you do not have the students' information available, ask the special education teacher to help you find this data in the students' IEP and planning and placement team minutes.

Teacher Tool

A listening center is an excellent tool to have, regardless of the subject you teach. Have relevant chapters from your textbooks on tape for students with learning disabilities to use. Recruit volunteers from parent or community groups to do the initial recording.

CONCLUDING THOUGHTS

When students with special needs are assigned to your classroom, you are required by law to make the modifications outlined in their IEPs. You can modify your program with minimal disruptions to ensure all students have a chance to learn regardless of their special needs by giving independent work in smaller segments; providing extra time to complete assignments; focusing on the objective you want the student to master; incorporating all learning modalities in the way you present information; having the students do simple exercises before writing;

modifying the assignments, if necessary; having a variety of multilevel books available; using graphic organizers; and keeping track of each student's objectives and modifications.

FOR FURTHER READING ON THIS SUBJECT

Byers, B. (2005). *Planning the curriculum for pupils with special educational needs: A practical guide (resource materials for teachers)* (2nd ed.). New York: David Fulton.

Lewis, R. B., & Doorlag, D. H. (2005). *Teaching special students in general education classrooms* (7th ed.). Upper Saddle River, NJ: Prentice Hall.

Winebrenner, S. (1996). *Teaching kids with learning difficulties in the regular classroom: Strategies and techniques every teacher can use to challenge and motivate struggling students.* Minneapolis, MN: Free Spirit.

19

Full-Inclusion Mainstreaming

Aliya was assigned a student with learning disabilities. Unlike her other mainstreamed students, this student was scheduled for full-inclusion mainstreaming and would not be pulled out for any special assistance. His most recent IEP stated he would benefit most by being in a general education classroom all day; however, Aliya did not have special education training besides the general information she'd received in one of her university courses. She was unsure what to do.*

Grade Levels

1–12

Timeline

All year, but especially the first month with these students

The Issue

What can I, as a non-special education teacher, do to adapt my program for a full-inclusion mainstreamed student?

---

*Basic ideas in this chapter contributed by Melodie Bitter, Lorne Street School, Los Angeles, California.

THE IDEA

Full inclusion means that the student with special needs is with a general education class and teacher for the entire day; the student isn't pulled out of class and doesn't receive any extra assistance, except perhaps the help of a temporary support assistant (TSA). Some students are ready to attend general education classes; others require more individual attention to be successful. Full-inclusion mainstreaming is the ultimate goal for all students in special education, and it is the general education teacher's responsibility to implement it. Following are ideas for ensuring your success and the success of all students, including full-inclusion students and the remainder of the class:

- Know your responsibilities.
- Use what you already know.
- Remember that you and the student's assistant are a team.
- Communicate with the parents.

KNOW THE CLASSROOM TEACHER'S RESPONSIBILITIES

Full-inclusion students are often assigned a TSA, popularly referred to as a one-on-one aide. Many teachers falsely assume that the TSA will take care of all behavioral problems with the student and the classroom teacher will not be involved. This is not true. The full-inclusion student is part of the regular classroom, and the teacher is totally responsible for the student. The TSA is there only for support.

The teacher is responsible for the student's education, resolving any academic or behavioral problems, and adhering to the student's IEP goals and objectives. The TSA provides extra assistance for the student to ensure his or her academic and social success. The TSA can help read and explain the material or transcribe oral responses to a test. In severe cases, the TSA can remove the student from the classroom when behavior warrants such measures.

USE WHAT YOU ALREADY KNOW

In teaching the full-inclusion student, use the same concepts that have been suggested in previous chapters, such as fairness, consistency, promotion of self-esteem, creativity, and so forth. These students are like all others in most ways. The only difference is that they have a disability in some area that must be addressed.

Study the student's IEP to learn about the disability and what you are to adapt to meet the student's educational needs. This is an important point because more often than not, the TSA has no experience doing this job. You are the one who is legally responsible for determining how to approach the student's learning experiences within the specific guidelines outlined in the IEP.

YOU AND THE STUDENT'S ASSISTANT ARE A TEAM

It is essential that you and the TSA work together as a team. At the beginning of the year, review with the TSA your expectations for the student to ensure that both of you respond to the student in the same fashion. Otherwise, the student will learn how to play one off of the other. Consistency will improve the student's behavior and academic achievement.

For example, if the assistant starts interacting with the class or giving ideas while sitting next to the student with special needs in a small group, the group may stop thinking and defer to the assistant. The TSA should also not be giving praise unless you have agreed on how the interaction with other students should be conducted.

> The full-inclusion student is part of the regular classroom, and the teacher is totally responsible for the student.

COMMUNICATE WITH THE PARENTS

Parents of students who are in a full-inclusion program are most often very involved in their child's education. Help the parents to be a part of the educational process in your room by keeping them informed.

It is recommended that the TSA be responsible for maintaining a daily anecdotal record to be sent home and signed by the parent. In this way, the parent will know daily what is happening in the classroom. These written records will help both the teacher and the parent to identify specific problem patterns, if any, and academic needs. They will also be beneficial as reference guides at future IEP meetings.

CONCLUDING THOUGHTS

Many students in special education are becoming identified as full-inclusion students. In these situations, you as the classroom teacher are responsible for their education whether or not you have had adequate training. You are responsible for implementing the goals and objectives of each student's IEP. In addition, you and the student's assistant must work as a team, while constantly communicating with the parents to ensure their support.

FOR FURTHER READING ON THIS SUBJECT

Hammeker, P. A. (2007). *The teacher's guide to inclusive education: 750 strategies for success.* Thousand Oaks, CA: Corwin.

McGrath, C. (2007). *The inclusion-classroom problem solver: Structures and supports to serve all learners.* Portsmouth, NH: Heinemann.

Nevin, A. I., & Villa, R. A. (2008). *A guide to co-teaching with paraeducators: Practical tips for K–12 educators.* Thousand Oaks, CA: Corwin.

20

Students With
ADD/ADHD and
Classroom Management

Aliya had a student who was diagnosed with attention deficit hyperactivity disorder (ADHD). He was not on medication and, as a result, was a continual disruption in the classroom. Her regular classroom management procedures did not work with him. What could she do?*

Grade Levels

K–8

Timeline

All year, but especially the first month

The Issue

How can I modify my classroom procedures for students with severe behavioral problems?

---

*Basic ideas in this chapter contributed by Jean Roberts, retired teacher, Hudson's Hope, British Columbia, Canada.

THE IDEA

If a student is identified as ADD or ADHD and is on medication to correct the problem, then you should treat the student no differently from any other student. The ADD/ADHD should not be an excuse for misbehavior because the medication and dosage should counteract the symptoms. The situation is similar to that of a nearsighted student who needs glasses. With the glasses, the student can function normally and is treated normally. A student with ADD/ADHD who is on correct medication should be able to function normally and should be treated like any other student.

Unfortunately, there is such a stigma attached to ADD/ADHD medication in our society that many parents refuse to use it with their children. As a result, many students are not medicated, and the teacher must deal with behaviors that the student often cannot control.

It is important to remember students with ADD/ADHD do not mean to misbehave. They have a chemical deficiency that often results in impulsive behavior, which the student often regrets immediately after it occurs.

The following tips may be helpful in dealing with students who have ADD/ADHD or other behavioral problems. Many of these tips are adaptations of concepts covered in earlier chapters:

- *Create class rules that are clear, concise, positive, and few in number.* Consequences must be immediate and easily enforced. Change positive consequences often, so they do not lose their motivational effect. Give the students their own personal copies of the rules to keep in their notebooks.
- *Provide a written schedule of daily events.* Avoid changes in the daily routine, if possible, and also avoid waiting periods between lessons. The students' attention spans are extremely short, and these periods are when behavioral problems arise.
- *Get the students' attention before giving instructions.* Keep the instructions clear, specific, and simple. If you are not sure that the students understand them, have them repeat the instructions. Also avoid putting an instruction in the form of a question such as "Would you . . . ?" or "Could you . . . ?" Say instead, "Please put the book back on the shelf."
- *Create hand signals for simple instructions.* Develop a secret signal, such as raising your hand for "stop," to remind the child not to blurt out answers. Other examples are pointing to your eye for "look" and to your ear for "listen."
- *Have shorter work periods for this child, and break assignments into smaller segments.* This does not mean reduce the work, but adapt the work to the student's shorter attention span.
- *Give the child a reason to move around.* This can entail running errands, helping in the classroom, handing out papers, cleaning the board, and so forth.
- *Allow a transition period after recess and lunchtime.* This will enable the student to mentally prepare for the next work period.
- *To decrease disorganization, keep materials at a minimum.* Students with ADD/ADHD are often quite disorganized. Distribute educational materials as needed.

- *Seat the student near you and away from distracting places*, for example, high-traffic areas such as the pencil sharpener. Decrease moving visual distractions.
- *Use a daily teacher-parent notebook to keep the parents informed.* This way you can communicate about daily problems, homework, good behavior, and so forth, and the parents can keep you informed of medication changes, home problems, and other relevant information.

Teacher Tool

Students with ADHD are especially difficult for substitute teachers, for their presence is a severe break from the normal routine for the student. Therefore, provide positive suggestions for substitute teachers. If possible, meet with the students before an absence to prepare them and decide on a positive consequence if the substitute gives them a good report.

- *If possible, always establish eye contact with the child.* Do not force it, however, as the child may concentrate on the eye contact and not on what is being said.
- *Use a balance of positive and negative consequences.* Too often the student with ADD/ADHD receives far more negative feedback than positive.
- *Be creative: Break up monotony with a variety of materials and presentations.* Try to structure activities so the students go from quiet to active ones.
- *Allow the use of a calculator, especially to check answers on math assignments.* This will enable the student with ADD/ADHD to catch mistakes made because of insufficient attention span for concentration and correcting mistakes. Also allow the student to use a typewriter, word processor, or computer, if necessary.

CONCLUDING THOUGHTS

Students with severe behavioral problems, such as those caused by unmedicated ADD/ADHD, need to have the class environment altered slightly to meet their needs and to help them succeed within an educational program. You can adapt your classroom in many small ways that often will benefit all students, including providing clear, consistent rules and a daily written schedule; getting the students' attention before instructing; keeping instructions clear, specific, and simple, and not putting them in the form of a question; creating hand signals for simple instructions; giving the child shorter work periods; finding ways for the child to move around periodically; allowing a transition period after recess and lunchtime; handing out materials only as needed; using a teacher-parent notebook; establishing eye contact with the child; balancing positive and negative consequences; being creative in your teaching; and allowing students with ADD/ADHD to use calculators, computers, and other tools as necessary.

FOR FURTHER READING ON THIS SUBJECT

Parker, H. C. (2001). *Problem solver guide for students with ADHD: Ready-to-use interventions for elementary and secondary students*. Plantation, FL: Specialty Press/A.D.D. Warehouse.

Pierangelo, R., & Giuliani, G. A. (2007). *Classroom management techniques for students with ADHD: A step-by-step guide for educators*. Thousand Oaks, CA: Corwin.

Rief, S. F. (2005). *How to reach & teach children with ADD/ADHD: Practical techniques, strategies & interventions*. San Francisco: Jossey-Bass.

21

Preparing for a Special Education Class

One of Aliya's best friends got a job as a special education teacher. As the two of them talked, Aliya discovered that her friend had received no more direction than she had in how to set up her educational program. Worse still, her friend's was the only full-day learning-disabled special education classroom in the building, so she had virtually no one to go to for direction. To exacerbate the situation, her friend would not be assigned a mentor teacher until the school year got under way. What could she do to survive those first few weeks?*

Grade Levels

K–12

Timeline

The week before school begins

The Issue

What do I need to do to organize a special education class?

---

*Basic ideas in this chapter contributed by Melodie Bitter, Lorne Street School, Los Angeles, California.

THE IDEA

Unfortunately, because of teacher shortages, more and more teachers are being assigned to special education classes without a great deal of training in this area. Whereas much of what a general education teacher knows about education is applicable to these situations, there are many significant differences.

The following ideas are geared toward multigrade classrooms for students who are learning handicapped or emotionally disturbed, but they supplement those already shared throughout this book. These important tips are for the new special education teacher at the beginning of the school year, regarding the following:

- The physical classroom arrangement
- Bulletin boards
- Classroom introductions
- The top four tips for success
- The first days

THE PHYSICAL CLASSROOM ARRANGEMENT

Arrange desks so that each student has his or her own personal desk. At first, there should be no sharing or grouping, as this leads to distractions. Students in special education need to learn how to function independently and focus on the work. (Most learn well how to avoid work, especially by interacting with others.) In addition, this arrangement gives the teacher or classroom aide more privacy and space for conducting one-on-one assistance.

Place the teacher's and aide's desks at opposite ends of the classroom, front and back, for supervision purposes and to create less disturbance if both adults are working with individual students.

BULLETIN BOARDS

As in general education classrooms, some bulletin boards in special education classrooms should be reserved for the students' work, and others should center on topics that are being taught at that time. Curricular boards are very important because the child with special needs in particular may require intellectual stimulation in a number of modalities, more so than other students.

CLASSROOM INTRODUCTIONS

On the first day, review three important items with your students in special education:

- *Classroom Responsibilities:* These are not rules, but responsibilities that every person in the class is expected to uphold. Too often students in special education become immediately resistant to a list of rules.
- *School Standards:* It is important to review the school standards with these students, to make them feel more like a part of the overall school and that they are being held accountable for the same standards as the general education students.
- *Personal Expectations:* This last part is very important. Too often previous teachers have had low personal expectations for these students, and as a result, the students have low expectations for themselves and therefore little academic and behavioral success. When your personal expectations are high (but realistic), the students will raise themselves to your expectations! This self-fulfilling prophecy is extremely strong with students in special education; they will inevitably raise or lower their work and behavior to your expectations.

Depending on the age of the students, you may want to include a discussion of your expectations for the overall year. Students in special education need to be especially clear about the choices they make, and the positive and negative consequences of those choices.

Teacher Tool

Arrange areas in various parts of the room where students can go when they complete their individual work so that they do not disturb others. These areas can house fun and educational activities such as puzzles, picture books with content appropriate to the reading level of the student, learning games such as GeoSafari, and other hands-on material.

The Top Four Tips for Success

Overall, there are four basic tips for achieving success in a special education classroom during that first month of school:

1. Always plan for more than you'll get through in a day. Sometimes, some of your ideas don't work with these particular kids on that particular day. Be prepared to switch to plan B. Also, with high expectations, your students may do better than you expected, and finish sooner than expected!

2. Be prepared to think on your feet. These students are often extremely intelligent and expect to be taken to areas you may not have anticipated, especially those with a behavioral disability. On the reverse side, a discipline or learning problem that unexpectedly develops could destroy a lesson for the entire class if not dealt with immediately and appropriately.

3. Be flexible. On some days, you may have to abandon your plans and do something else. That's okay and part of being a special education teacher!

4. Finally, and probably most important, enjoy your students. These are usually sweet, fun kids, and a good special education teacher can have an immense impact on their future.

THE FIRST DAYS

There are a number of items requiring your immediate attention in a special education classroom. Whereas all are also applicable to a general education classroom, they are critically important in the special education classroom:

- *Placement Tests:* Begin the first day by administering a placement test. Try to have all the tests completed by the third day. The sooner the students are on a regular routine, the better they will respond.
- *Nonacademic Activities:* Plan to include some nonacademic, or fun, activities for the first day along with the academic. Provide time for interaction. Students may play games, work on a fun assignment together, or whatever you decide. It is important not to rely on just academic or just nonacademic on the first day, for this sets the tone of and expectations for the remainder of the school year.
- *Physical Education:* In an elementary school, plan for physical education to begin immediately. Tremendous social skills, along with physical skills, a sense of classroom cohesion, and organizational skills are developed on the playground, especially for the students in special education.

CONCLUDING THOUGHTS

In many respects, organizing a special education class is similar to organizing a traditional classroom; however, there are some significant differences. These include the necessity of special planning for the physical classroom arrangement, the bulletin boards, classroom introductions, and the first couple of days. It is also important for the new special education teacher to keep in mind the top four tips for success: Always plan for more than you'll need, be prepared to think on your feet, be flexible, and, most important, enjoy your students.

FOR FURTHER READING ON THIS SUBJECT

DeBettencourt, L. U., & Howard, L. A. (2006). *The effective special education teacher: A practical guide for success.* Upper Saddle River, NJ: Prentice Hall.

Pierangelo, R., & Giuliani, G. A. (2008). *Teaching in a special education classroom: A step-by-step guide for educators.* Thousand Oaks, CA: Corwin.

Ysseldyke, J., & Algozzine, R. (2006). *A practical approach to special education for every teacher: The 13 book collection.* Thousand Oaks, CA: Corwin.

PART VI

How to Maintain Your Sanity

✓ **Making It Through Your Teacher Evaluation**

How can I alleviate the stress of my formal teaching evaluations?

✓ **Ten Ways to Avoid Stress**

How can I alleviate my first-year teaching stress?

✓ **Putting It All Into Perspective**

How do I keep in mind why I chose to be a teacher?

22

Making It Through Your Teacher Evaluation

Aliya's principal informed her that she was going to be observed for a formal evaluation that day. She was extremely nervous. Although her experienced peers told her that she had done fairly well throughout the year for a first-year teacher, she was deathly afraid of what the principal would say—or possibly do—after the evaluation. She taught her lesson, the students were well behaved, but she constantly stressed every time she noticed the principal writing on his pad of paper. She was told she would be formally observed at least three more times that year. What could she do to alleviate the stress these observations were causing her?

Grade Levels

K–12

Timeline

All year, but especially around the time when the administration conducts formal observations

The Issue

How can I alleviate the stress of my formal teaching evaluations?

THE IDEA

All teachers are formally evaluated by the administration as part of the education code of every state. Experienced teachers may be evaluated every two to five years. However, new teachers can expect to be formally observed several times during their first few years until they achieve "permanent" or "tenured" status.

The stress that you will feel is mostly self-inflicted. It is set up by your fear that you will do poorly, your principal or administrator will not like you, and ultimately, you will lose your job. That is not the healthiest or most helpful mindset to have. To alleviate this mental pressure, you need to start by remembering the primary rule about administrative evaluations:

The administrators are not the enemy—They want you to succeed!

This is especially true if the administrator hired you.

Think about it—there are very good and highly logical reasons for the administrators to want you to succeed:

- Your success makes the school better and raises the school's test scores.
- They hired you—your success shows everyone that they know how to hire good teachers.
- It is a major time-consuming hassle to make a case in the effort to get rid of a poor teacher—even one who is new.

A much healthier mindset is for you to welcome administrators into your classroom. This is an excellent time to "show off" how good you really are as a teacher!

THE OBSERVATION

Ideally, there should be a pre-observation conference where you can discuss what the lesson is, how it relates to standards and curriculum, and what instructional strategies are best suited. Unfortunately, due to time constraints and administrative workloads, this phase of the evaluation is usually omitted. Very often, the evaluation event starts when the administrator enters your room.

Here are some basic ideas that you should follow during the formal observation:

- *Have a classroom greeter.* This can be used all through the year, not just during administrator observations. When an adult enters the room, the classroom greeter immediately welcomes (quietly) the visitor, asking them, "How can I help you?" If the person is there to observe (for whatever reason), the greeter informs the visitor as to what the class is currently doing. Not only does a classroom greeter limit interruptions in your teaching, but it gives an excellent first impression to any visitors, including administrators.

- *Provide the administrator with a copy of your lesson plan.* If you know about the observation in advance, you can have a copy prepared. If not, give the administrator your personal lesson plan. Don't make a big deal out of it—don't stop to explain where you are in the lesson. The administrator should be able to figure that out. Just continue your lesson without interruption as you walk over and hand the administrator your lesson plan. Even if you have a lesson plan for the administrator, you should have an agenda on the board that gives a brief summary of what is being covered that period. This is especially important if the administrator comes in for a quick informal evaluation and wants a quick idea of what is occurring in the lesson.
- *Show them what they want to see.* Every year, the administration will usually key in on certain aspects of education in which they want to see more of a focus. These areas could entail increasing literacy across the curriculum, expanding the use of cooperative learning, the integration of certain technologies, or a whole host of ideas. Their focus may be explicit—the administrators will tell you exactly what they want to see. Their focus may be implicit—specific directions are not stated, but the majority of inservice workshops revolve around one or two specific topics. Either way, it behooves you to ensure that you plan on showing them what they want to see. The following are examples:
  o If you know about the observation in advance, directly implement the administration's area of focus into your lesson plan.
  o If you do not know about the observation in advance, try to adapt your lesson so that it includes their area of focus in some fashion (called "thinking on your feet").
  o If the observation is not planned in advance and it is not practical to include the administrative area of focus at that time, be sure to mention how it fits into your overall unit of which the observed lesson was a part.

It is also critical that you understand that the administrator is *not* only looking at your teaching! Other areas that will be observed at some point are as follows:

- *What are the students doing?* Are they actively engaged? Are they off-task? How do they relate to the teacher?
- *What is the room environment?* Does it support the curricula? Is it conducive to a positive learning environment? Is it clean and organized?

Formal evaluations are normally followed by an official conference where the administrator shares thoughts and observations and offers you assistance. This part is often more stressful for the teacher than the actual observation. However, if you go in with the mind-set promoted above—that the administrator is there to help you and wants you to succeed—then the conference should be beneficial.

THE POST-OBSERVATION CONFERENCE

Here are some basic ideas that you should follow during your post-observation conference:

- *Listen and don't be defensive.* The tendency for teachers during a post-observation conference is to attempt to immediately explain anything that was questioned by the administrator. More often than not, you come off as being highly defensive. Sit quietly and listen, and only explain why you did what you did when asked. Often the administrator was simply telling you what was observed. If the administrator wants to know your reasoning for something, you will be asked.
- *Responding to "How do you feel the lesson went?"* One of the most used questions that an administrator will ask at the start of a post-observation conference is "How do you feel the lesson went?" Too often the teacher answers what they think the administrator wants to hear (positive, negative, or purposely ambiguous) rather than a truthful self-analysis. Administrators want to know that you have a realistic view of your teaching and that you can conduct an honest self-evaluation. Therefore, if you are asked how you felt the lesson went, be honest and specific, using actual examples from the session. If something went well, be specific and explain why. If something did not go well, again, be specific, tell what you think was the cause and how you would improve it in the future. The administrator knows you will make mistakes because you are new. It is much more important to know that you can recognize mistakes and figure out ways to improve.
- *Take feedback.* Do not only listen to what is being said, but take notes and plan on following through with the suggestions. This is important even if you may not totally agree with the advice. Remember—you are new. The administrator started in the classroom. Even if the person has not taught for many years, the administrator regularly observes other teachers and knows good teaching techniques. You may pick up some good tips. However, if you are adamantly opposed to one of the suggestions, be prepared to share your reasoning, using good objective, unemotional arguments, and relating it directly to your perception of the students' achievement.
- *Keep a copy of any written observation feedback.* If you are provided any paperwork on the observation, keep a copy of it in a folder. This could be important at a final, summative evaluation meeting, especially if you have multiple administrators observing you throughout the year. If the particular observation was basically negative, even if you explained yourself in a conference, write a memorandum to the administrator putting your explanations in writing and keep a copy. Consult with your union representative on what and how to write your memo.

It is also important to note that you do not need to wait for an administrator to initiate an observation. You can, and should, invite your administrator into your classroom whenever you are doing something special or impressive. Administrators enjoy seeing good teaching. Having them in your room on a regular basis not only shows off what an asset you are to the school, but will make you more comfortable and stress-free when they have to come in for a formal evaluative observation.

CONCLUDING THOUGHTS

The first thing to do in alleviating the stress of a formal evaluative observation is to remember that the administrator is coming in wanting you to succeed. During the observation, have a classroom greeter provide the administrator with a copy of your lesson plan, and be sure to show the administrator what he or she wants to see. During the subsequent post-observation conference, listen and don't be defensive, know how to answer the question "How do you feel the lesson went?" take feedback, and keep a copy of any written observation feedback. Be sure to also invite administrators into your classroom throughout the year to observe anything special or impressive you have planned. By following these ideas, you will become more comfortable with observers and find your stress level reduced during formal evaluative observations.

FOR FURTHER READING ON THIS SUBJECT

Airasian, P. W. (1996). *Teacher self-evaluation tool kit.* Thousand Oaks, CA: Corwin.

Danielson, C. (2007). *Enhancing professional practice: A framework for teaching* (2nd ed.). Alexandria, VA: Association for Supervision and Curriculum Development.

Wyatt, R. L., III, & Looper, S. (2003). *So you have to have a portfolio: A teacher's guide to preparation and presentation* (2nd ed.). Thousand Oaks, CA: Corwin.

23

Ten Ways to Avoid Stress

By February, Aliya was beginning to question whether she had made the right career decision. She was frustrated by all the responsibilities she had, in addition to learning ways to teach and how to handle the students and the paperwork. Her weeks had been filled with staying up until midnight grading papers, no time for her family, overeating one week, undereating the next, and insomnia. She was very stressed out and didn't know what to do. Was there any hope?*

Grade Levels

K–12

Timeline

All year, but especially around the third through the seventh month

The Issue

How can I alleviate my first-year teaching stress?

---

*Basic ideas in this chapter contributed by Tony Murphy, O'Connell Secondary School, Dublin, Ireland.

THE IDEA

New teachers, like all professionals, feel stressed during the first year of employment. Stress management books, however, are rarely geared to the unique situations confronting a new teacher on a daily basis. Take heart: The experiences of your senior peers have evolved into the following ten effective ways to reduce stress.

- *Be prepared.* An essential part of the job, lesson preparation markedly reduces anxiety. To know in your mind what you are going to do during the class period eliminates having to plan while presenting the material. It enables you to deal with the unpredictable, for the unexpected *will* happen. Being prepared with optional approaches allows for flexibility. Also remember that no one has a good day every day, and you will not be able to give 100% on some days. As the leader in the classroom, have an alternate plan to implement when the need arises. For example, prepare special worksheets or a specific activity to accompany a video or audio recording you have on hand for such situations.
- *Know and understand the material you are teaching.* Personally do all homework and tests before you assign or explain them. Being in command of your subject is a great boost to the students' confidence in you as the instructional leader. You do not want to become suddenly stuck while demonstrating a math problem on the board. If you do not know an answer, however, be honest and say so with the proviso you will look it up for the next day.

> **Teacher Tool**
>
> Use shortcuts to reduce the time you spend on paperwork, such as a computer to store recurring material that you can cut and paste instead of rewrite or retype. Ask other teachers what shortcuts they use.

- *Keep your paperwork up to date.* In addition to teaching, teachers have a flow of record-keeping responsibilities that has become the bane of the profession. These records must be kept up to date and accurate. Falling behind and allowing the paperwork to accumulate can be a great source of stress. Make a schedule of what needs to be done and when.
- *Decide what to grade, what not to grade.* New teachers can be overwhelmed with the amount of grading—especially secondary teachers who may see 150–200 different students in one day. Not everything has to be graded. Decide what is important, what papers demonstrate the students' mastery of the standards and information. These get graded. Practice papers, such as most homework, can be graded in class or by the student's peers. Some papers can simply be marked with a check mark as completed. If you try to grade everything, you may discover you will have no life of your own.

- *Seek advice from experienced teachers.* Choose wisely. Advice from teachers and administrators tends to fall into three categories. First is the "ignore it at your peril" advice that comes from your administrator or department chair. Follow this at all costs. Then there is the advice that is offered whether or not you want it. This kind can be listened to politely and forgotten. Genuinely useful advice comes in response to a question from you. Sharing a difficulty helps make it seem less of a problem, for a trouble shared is a trouble halved. You will learn that your classroom experiences are not unique, and others have successfully resolved them. That information will help you resolve your issues.
- *Seek advice from friends who are also new teachers.* New teachers are experiencing the same problems you are. Maintaining the attention of a class may be second nature to an experienced teacher. Experienced teachers may not even be aware of the new and innovative techniques that are being used to motivate students. Your peers probably have encountered the same problem as you and may have found a solution already. The sharing of solutions will help, but even if no one has a good solution, simply knowing you are not alone and that others have similar issues reduces your own doubts and is a positive reinforcement.

> New teachers who never fail in their lessons are the ones who will rarely try anything new or innovative.

- *Make a list of what you hope to accomplish in a day or throughout the week.* This can be very useful in reducing the strain. When you complete an item, strike it. This will provide great self-satisfaction. Don't, however, expect to get through every point on your list. Be sure to prioritize those things that absolutely must get done that day. Incorporate last week's list into your new one and recognize the time restrictions this week.
- *Encourage students to be independent.* Suggest that the more able among them work on their own (on appropriate material, such as extra credit, other assignments, enrichment, or their own projects) when they have completed their assigned work. This can help take the strain of finding extra work for them off your shoulders.
- *Talk to colleagues about recreational activities.* Do not restrict your conversation to school items and avoid becoming isolated. Socialize with your colleagues. Too often new teachers spend all day in their rooms. One needs a mental break. Participate in faculty functions (such as the Friday happy hour). Be sure that you always plan time for yourself and your family. If you grade papers all weekend, you'll come in on Monday and yell at the students.
- *Accept your mistakes.* Mistakes are learning experiences. Do not spend hours worrying about "if only I had acted differently," or "if only I had not said what I said." New teachers who never fail in their lessons are the ones who will rarely try anything new or innovative.

Many new teachers, at the end of their first year, felt that working harder did not decrease their stress levels. Obviously what works for these new teachers might not work for you, for reasons of personality, situation, age, and so on, but they may be worth a try in this difficult first year—before reaching for the tranquilizers.

CONCLUDING THOUGHTS

One of the most important things that you can do to survive your first year is learn how to control stress. This can be accomplished by thoroughly preparing your lesson and ensuring you know the material. In addition, always keep paperwork up to date. Always know your students as individuals. Seek advice from both the experienced and new teachers to eliminate feelings of isolation. Make a list of things to do on a weekly basis.

Always encourage student academic independence. Enjoy recreational activities with colleagues and with family, leave your stress and personal problems at the classroom door, and know that it is okay to make mistakes.

FOR FURTHER READING ON THIS SUBJECT

DeAmicis, B. (2001). *3 cheers for teaching*. Chicago: Zephyr Press.

Martin, K., & Brenny, K. (2005). *1000 best new teacher survival secrets*. Naperville, IL: Sourcebooks.

Queen, J. A., & Queen, P. S. (2003). *The frazzled teacher's wellness plan: A five step program for reclaiming time, managing stress, and creating a healthy lifestyle*. Thousand Oaks, CA: Corwin.

24

Putting It All Into Perspective

By the end of the school year, Aliya wasn't sure she would be returning. She completed the year with excellent evaluations, but she was unsure if teaching was still the "noble calling" she had first expected. Then something happened. She had a breakthrough with one of her problem students, one whom she could not get through to all year. And at the end of the year when he thanked her and gave her an unsolicited hug, she remembered why she had chosen to be a teacher.

Grade Levels

K–12

Timeline

All year, but especially around the third through the seventh month

The Issue

How do I keep in mind why I chose to be a teacher?

THE IDEA

During your first year of teaching, you may wonder, "Why am I doing this?" To help you remember why you are a teacher, and why you continue teaching, consider the memorable teaching moments in this chapter submitted by teachers from around the country.

They were posed the question, "What is your most memorable teaching moment?" Some of their responses concerned students, some parents. Most were wonderful experiences; a couple were not. But all of the experiences reminded these teachers of why they went into this profession, and why they stay in it, throughout all the trials and tribulations. (Note: Names are omitted to protect the privacy of students and parents in the stories.)

As you go through your teaching career, you will also accumulate special moments like these. Enjoy them. They are why we do this job.

CONCLUDING THOUGHTS

As you think about all of the frustration and stress associated with your first year of teaching, there's one thing you need to always keep in mind: why you became a teacher.

MEMORABLE TEACHING MOMENTS

Last year, my co-teacher and I shared a group of 45 seventh grade students in a team-teaching setting. We had a very close relationship with this group of students as the year progressed. We learned early in the year about one of our students and his economic strife and decided that at the holidays we would take care of many of his needs that were not being met economically. We purchased a coat, gloves, hat, back-pack, binder, art materials (he loves to work in a variety of media), and a few games. We wrapped them in holiday paper, and so as not to embarrass him, we set up a plan to have these gifts anonymously awaiting him in the psychologist's office, where he often visited.

The psychologist came to us later in the day filled with obvious emotion. He told us that he only wished we could have seen the joy on this student's face as he literally leaped through the office and skipped through the halls. He was so excited. To this day, I don't believe this young man knows the secret of the gift, but he still comes to visit. It was (and still is) such a good feeling.

❖

Early in my career, I had started teaching third grade in a low-income school in not the greatest of neighborhoods. One of my students was constantly late for school. It was very frustrating for me as a teacher because he was losing valuable instructional time. One day he walked in very late and I had come to the end of my rope. I looked him in the eyes and said,

"You need to start being on time to school. The next time you are late, I am going to refer you to the office." The child looked at me and said, "But it wasn't my fault."

After going around and around about responsibility, he finally threw his arms up in the air and said, "I couldn't leave the house because there were gunshots." I felt like the worst person on the face of the earth. Needless to say, I excused the tardy.

What did I learn from all of this? You need to find out all the information before jumping to conclusions. Things are not always what they seem.

One of my kindergarten girls brought a book from home and announced that she wanted to read it to the class. Now I knew she couldn't read, so I was trying tactfully to put her off. When the principal stopped by the room to observe a little later, the student invited her to the reading. The principal said she would love to come and I apprehensively set a time. At the appointed time, the class and the principal was seated attentively. The student held up the book and announced the title just as she had seen me do before. She licked her fingers and turned to the first page of the story. At this point, she looked up and said, "I forgot! I don't know how to read!"

One of my most memorable teaching experiences involved three large rocks and a little girl who did the best she could. Each week one of my third graders would take home the "estimation jar" and fill it with items that we would use to estimate with in math. Most students brought candy, cookies, marshmallows, and so forth that could be shared with the class after the lesson. One girl who didn't get much help at home brought in three big rocks inside the jar. The other students made fun of her because it was too easy to guess that she had brought three rocks. Seeing that the girl was embarrassed and hurt, I quickly went into action. I asked students to come up with ways we could estimate with the rocks. I got out the scales, string, rulers, and so forth, and we estimated and compared the size and weight of those three rocks using many math skills. We went far beyond the lesson I had planned for the day. We all learned a great deal from a math lesson on three large rocks. The smile and the hug I got from that little girl as she left that day added icing to the cake.

I teach first grade in a rural, economically disadvantaged school. One parent, in determination to help her child do well in school, often came to class to meet with me after school. I soon realized this parent could not read. The most memorable moment came at the end of the year, when she read me a thank-you note that she had written herself.

My very first year of teaching, the first day of the second semester, I had two remedial classes that tried my soul. In one class was a tall, good-looking, charming, and totally disruptive eighth grader named Gabriel. I worked hard to help Gabriel find some meaning in school, but he did not pass my class.

The next year, Gabriel, as a ninth grader, burst into my room one afternoon and knocked another boy out cold. Gabriel was expelled, and I did not see him for several years. One afternoon, I was late leaving for home, and a lone handball player suddenly stopped as I passed. He called, "Hey, it's me! Gabriel! Do you remember me?" I said I did, and asked him what he was up to. He told me that he was in continuation school. He had spent time in prison, but he was now better and was determined to get his diploma. Then he said, "You know, I'm sorry for what I did that day." I thanked him and went home, marveling at how he must have carried that with him all those years, and how gratifying and touching it was to hear those words!

This is my first year of teaching and I have never been more excited about anything in my life. Believe it or not one of my most memorable moments just happened the other day. One of my students had stayed to help me after class, and she went up to the podium. She was standing there and pointing her finger toward the board and mouthing something. I asked her what she was doing. She told me that she just wanted to see what it was like to be me. I knew at that moment that I was at the point in my life that I had dreamed about for so many years. She looked up to me as I had once looked up to my third-grade teacher.

My most memorable teaching moment was during the end of my first year of teaching. The freshman science class that had given me the hardest time in the beginning of the year found out when my birthday was and threw me a surprise party.

I received a strange call from one of the English teachers right before his class. The English teacher asked me to come to his room because he wanted me to be a witness when he called a parent. However, the story was fake, and the students wanted me out of the room while they set up posters, food, and drinks. I received lots of cards from them telling me how much they appreciated me!

Here's a story that reinforces the need for good preparation when teaching. It was my second year teaching and my school was doing a multicultural festival. Each class was researching and learning about a different culture.

I signed up to study Thailand because of my love for the cuisine. I had collected several books on Thailand and got started. My eager students were listening intently as I was reading information to them from one of the resources about the importance of rivers to the people of Thailand.

Unfortunately, I hadn't read the passage ahead of time and came to the name of an important river: "Phuket." Without thinking ahead, I tried to sound out the name as best as I could. As soon as I said it, however, I knew I was in trouble. You can imagine how my class sounded with their cheery voices mimicking my own pronunciation of this important river over and over. I will never forget the name of that river.

Alvin is a typical ELL first-grade student. He can speak English and can understand it, but he is still struggling with his vocabulary.

One day, he came back to school after an absence due to a cold. I heard someone sneeze, and when I turned around to check who it was, Alvin was right behind me asking, "Teacher, may I have a 'bless you'?" I gave him a whole box of tissues, plus a hug.

I ran into one of my difficult former special education students at the mall. He was eighteen years old and told me of his plans to be a truck driver. I asked what had sparked his interest. He said, "In fourth grade, you taught me about all the fifty states. You made them sound so cool, I wanted to see them all for myself." I didn't think I had made any impression on him, but I guess I did.

It was close to the beginning of the school year, and my kindergarten class was discussing family relationships. We had listed such relatives as grandmother, grandfather, mother, dad, brother, cousin, and so on. I was trying to pull the word "sister" from the class by saying, "What do you call that girl that lives with you at home who is not your mother?" From the back of the room comes a small male voice, "Rat!"

I was overworked and underpaid teaching technical theater. On a particular occasion, as had happened before, the sound system didn't work. As a student and I were wading through a mess of cables, cords, and plugs, I felt my frustration level reach the top. Just when I was about to give up, the student said, "This is so much fun! If it wasn't for this class, I would never want to come to school!"

My foods and nutrition students sliced, peeled, and carved away. We were preparing fruit trays in the lab when one of the high school boys asked, "If I plant the leftover seeds from the apples, will these grow?" Not being the agricultural expert, I referred him to another student whose family raised crops. Later, I found out how scarce food was in his household. I had never thought much about his thin body frame, attributing it to his being an active teenager. His father and siblings lived on the same rural road as my parents. The mother had left some years earlier. As I was driving by one day, I noticed these small apple trees growing among some other bushes. I began to feel guilty for not realizing his predicament earlier.

One day at lunch, he came by school after he graduated to see some of his former teachers. I had brought some leftovers from home consisting of pinto beans, fried potatoes and onions, and cornbread. I offered to share it with him, so we sat in the kitchen lab and caught up on his work and the group home in which he lived. I guess it touched me in a way that no other teaching situation has. Today, I am much more in tune to students' real hunger, not only for food but attention as well.

Further Reading

Airasian, P. W. (1996). *Teacher self-evaluation tool kit*. Thousand Oaks, CA: Corwin.

Anderson, L. W., Krathwohl, D. R., Airasian, P. W., Cruikshank, K. A., Mayer, R. E., Pintrich, P. R., et al. (Eds.). (2000). *A taxonomy for learning, teaching, and assessing: A revision of Bloom's taxonomy of educational objectives, abridged edition* (2nd ed.). Columbus, OH: Allyn & Bacon.

Bender, Y. (2004). *The power of positive teaching: 35 successful strategies for active and enthusiastic classroom participation*. White River Junction, VT: Nomad Press.

Bothmer, S. (2003). *Creating the peaceable classroom: Techniques to calm, uplift, and focus teachers and students*. Tucson, AZ: Zephyr Press.

Boult, B. (2006). *176 ways to involve parents: Practical strategies for partnering with families* (2nd ed.). Thousand Oaks, CA: Corwin.

Burchard, B. (2008). *The student leadership guide* (4th ed.). Garden City, NY: Morgan James.

Burke, K. (2006). *From standards to rubrics in six steps: Tools for assessing student learning, K–8*. Thousand Oaks, CA: Corwin.

Burke, K. (2008). *What to do with the kid who . . . : Developing cooperation, self-discipline, and responsibility in the classroom*. Thousand Oaks, CA: Corwin.

Byers, B. (2005). *Planning the curriculum for pupils with special educational needs: A practical guide (resource materials for teachers)* (2nd ed.). New York: David Fulton.

Corcoran, J. (2007). *First year teacher: Wisdom, warnings, and what I wish I'd known my first 100 days on the job*. New York: Kaplan.

Danielson, C. (2007). *Enhancing professional practice: A framework for teaching* (2nd ed.). Alexandria, VA: Association for Supervision and Curriculum Development.

DeAmicis, B. (2001). *3 cheers for teaching!* Chicago: Zephyr Press.

DeBettencourt, L. U., & Howard, L. A. (2006). *The effective special education teacher: A practical guide for success*. Upper Saddle River, NJ: Prentice Hall.

Ebiefung, A. (2002). *Responsible use of the Internet in education: Issues concerning evaluation, citation, copyright and fair use of web materials*. Cleveland, TN: Penman.

Evanski, G. A. (2008). *Classroom activities: More than 100 ways to energize learners* (2nd ed.). Thousand Oaks, CA: Corwin.

Glasgow, N. A., & Hicks, C. D. (2009). *What successful teachers do: 101 research-based classroom strategies for new and veteran teachers* (2nd ed.). Thousand Oaks, CA: Corwin.

Guskey, T. R. (2008). *Practical solutions for serious problems in standards-based grading*. Thousand Oaks, CA: Corwin.

Hammeker, P. A. (2007). *The teacher's guide to inclusive education: 750 strategies for success*. Thousand Oaks, CA: Corwin.

Hawthorne, K., & Gibson, J. E. (2002). *Bulletin board power: Bridges to lifelong learning*. Westport, CT: Libraries Unlimited.

Heiss, R. (2004). *Feng shui for the classroom: 101 easy-to-use ideas.* Chicago: Zephyr Press.

Kiewra, K. A. (2008). *Teaching how to learn: The teacher's guide to student success.* Thousand Oaks, CA: Corwin.

Kottler, J. A., & Kottler, E. (2006). *Counseling skills for teachers* (2nd ed.). Thousand Oaks, CA: Corwin.

Lawrence, D. (2006). *Enhancing self-esteem in the classroom* (3rd ed.). West Yorkshire, England: Paul Chapman.

Lazear, D. (1998). *The rubrics way: Using MI to assess understanding.* Chicago: Zephyr Press.

Lewis, R. B., & Doorlag, D. H. (2005). *Teaching special students in general education classrooms* (7th ed.). Upper Saddle River, NJ: Prentice Hall.

Mandel, S. (2003). *Cooperative work groups: Preparing students for the real world.* Thousand Oaks, CA: Corwin.

Mandel, S. (2006). *Improving test scores: A practical approach for teachers and administrators.* Thousand Oaks, CA: Corwin.

Mandel, S. (2007). *The parent-teacher partnership: How to work together for student achievement.* Chicago: Zephyr Press.

Martin, K., & Brenny, K. (2005). *1000 best new teacher survival secrets.* Naperville, IL: Sourcebooks.

McGrath, C. (2007). *The inclusion-classroom problem solver: Structures and supports to serve all learners.* Portsmouth, NH: Heinemann.

Mierzwik, D. (2005). *Classroom record keeping made simple: Tips for time-strapped teachers.* Thousand Oaks, CA: Corwin.

Mills, D. W. (Ed.). (2000). *Substitute teacher homepage: The substitute teacher survival site.* Retrieved February 23, 2009, from http://www.csrnet.org/csrnet/substitute.

Moran, C., Stobbe, J. C., Baron, W., Miller, J., & Moir, E. (2008). *Keys to the elementary classroom: A new teacher's guide to the first month of school* (3rd ed.). Thousand Oaks, CA: Corwin.

Nelson, J., Lott, L., & Glenn, H. S. (2000). *Positive discipline in the classroom: Developing mutual respect, cooperation, and responsibility in your classroom* (Rev. 3rd ed.). New York: Three Rivers Press.

Nelson, K. J. (2007). *Teaching in the digital age: Using the Internet to increase student engagement and understanding* (2nd ed.). Thousand Oaks, CA: Corwin.

Nevin, A. I., & Villa, R. A. (2008). *A guide to co-teaching with paraeducators: Practical tips for K–12 educators.* Thousand Oaks, CA: Corwin.

Parker, H. C. (2001). *Problem solver guide for students with ADHD: Ready-to-use interventions for elementary and secondary students.* Plantation, FL: Specialty Press/A.D.D. Warehouse.

Passatore, M. A. (1998). *Bulletin board? Or bulletin boards!* Landam, MD: Scarecrow Press.

Peltz, W. H. (2007). *Dear teacher: Expert advice for effective study skills.* Thousand Oaks, CA: Corwin.

Pierangelo, R., & Giuliani, G. A. (2007). *Classroom management techniques for students with ADHD: A step-by-step guide for educators.* Thousand Oaks, CA: Corwin.

Pierangelo, R., & Giuliani, G. A. (2008). *Teaching in a special education classroom: A step-by-step guide for educators.* Thousand Oaks, CA: Corwin.

Plummer, D. M. (2007). *Helping children to build self-esteem: A photocopiable activities book* (2nd ed.). Philadelphia: Jessica Kingsley.

Podesta, C. (2001). *Self-esteem and the 6-second secret.* Thousand Oaks, CA: Corwin.

Queen, J. A., & Queen, P. S. (2003). *The frazzled teacher's wellness plan: A five step program for reclaiming time, managing stress, and creating a healthy lifestyle.* Thousand Oaks, CA: Corwin.

Rief, S. F. (2005). *How to reach & teach children with ADD/ADHD: Practical techniques, strategies & interventions.* San Francisco: Jossey-Bass.

Robbins, K., & Schmitt, L. (2002). *Big bulletin boards: A cooperative approach* (2nd ed.). Seattle: Hide and Seek Press.

Rozakis, L. (2002). *Super study skills.* New York: Scholastic.

Rude, C. A. (2007). *How to succeed as a substitute teacher: Everything you need from start to finish.* Thousand Oaks, CA; Corwin.

Rudney, G. L. (2005). *Every teacher's guide to working with parents.* Thousand Oaks, CA: Corwin.

Smith, G. G., Latham, G., Longhurst, M. L., & Ditlevsen, M. (2004). *Substitute teacher handbook K–12* (6th ed.). Logan, UT: Substitute Teacher Workshop/Utah State University.

Smith, R. (2008). *Conscious classroom management: Unlocking the secrets of great teaching* (3rd ed.). Thousand Oaks, CA: Corwin.

Spiegel, D. L. (2005). *Classroom discussion: Strategies for engaging all students, building higher-level thinking skills, and strengthening reading and writing across the curriculum.* New York: Scholastic.

Stevens, D. D., & Levi, A. J. (2004). *Introduction to rubrics: An assessment tool to save grading time, convey effective feedback and promote student learning.* Sterling, VA: Stylus.

Tingley, S. C. (2006). *How to handle difficult parents: A teacher's survival guide.* Fort Collins, CO: Cottonwood Press.

Turville, J. (2007). *Differentiating by student interest: Strategies and lesson plans.* Larchmont, NY: Eye on Education.

Walsh, J. A., & Sattes, B. D. (2004). *Quality questioning: Research-based practice to engage every learner.* Thousand Oaks: CA: Corwin.

Winebrenner, S. (1996). *Teaching kids with learning difficulties in the regular classroom: Strategies and techniques every teacher can use to challenge and motivate struggling students.* Minneapolis, MN: Free Spirit.

Wolfe, S. (2006). *Your best year yet! A guide to purposeful planning and effective classroom organization.* Washington, DC: Teaching Strategies.

Wormeli, R. (2006). *Fair isn't always equal: Assessing & grading in the differentiated classroom.* Portland, ME: Stenhouse.

Wright, K. (2002). *Building school and community partnerships through parent involvement* (2nd ed.). Upper Saddle River, NJ: Prentice Hall.

Wyatt, R. L., III, & Looper, S. (2003). *So you have to have a portfolio: A teacher's guide to preparation and presentation* (2nd ed.). Thousand Oaks, CA: Corwin.

Ysseldyke, J., & Algozzine, R. (2006). *A practical approach to special education for every teacher: The 13 book collection.* Thousand Oaks, CA: Corwin.

References

Armstrong, T. (2000). *Multiple intelligences in the classroom.* Alexandria, VA: Association for Supervision and Curriculum Development.

Bloom, B. S. (Ed.). (1953). *Taxonomy of educational objectives: Handbook 1: Cognitive domain.* New York: David McKay.

Daly, J. A., & Suite, A. (1981). Classroom seating choice and teacher perceptions of students. *Journal of Experimental Education, 50,* 64–69.

Hinduja, S., & Patchin, J. W. (2008). *Bullying beyond the schoolyard: Preventing and responding to cyberbullying.* Thousand Oaks, CA: Corwin.

Mandel, S. (1991). *Responses to cooperative learning processes among elementary age students.* Unpublished doctoral dissertation, University of Southern California. (ERIC Document Reproduction Service No. ED332808).

Mandel, S. (2003). *Cooperative work groups: Preparing students for the real world.* Thousand Oaks, CA: Corwin.

Mandel, S. (2006). *Improving test scores: A practical approach for teachers and administrators.* Thousand Oaks, CA: Corwin.

Mandel, S. (2007). *The parent-teacher partnership: How to work together for student achievement.* Chicago: Zephyr Press.

Margulies, N. (with Maal, N.). (2002). *Mapping inner space: Learning and teaching visual mapping* (2nd ed.). Tucson, AZ: Zephyr Press.

Paine, S. C. (1983). *Structuring your classroom for academic success.* Champaign, IL.: Research Press.

Index

Activities, sponge, 12
Administrators and teacher evaluations, 107–111
Advice from other teachers, 114
Agendas, daily, 13
Alta Vista Babel Fish Translation, 84
Arrangement of classrooms, 8–9, 15–17
  for special education classes, 103
Attention deficit disorder (ADD), 52–53, 82
  classroom management of students with, 98–101
Attention deficit hyperactivity disorder (ADHD), 52–53, 82
  classroom management of students with, 98–101
Attention signals, 11, 99

Back to School Night, 81, 82
Beginning of the year questionnaires, 82
Behavior, negative student, 51–54, 119
Bell schedules, 9
Best of History Web Sites, 48
Binders, substitute teacher, 22–24
Bloom, Benjamin, 29
Bloom's taxonomy, 29–30
Boards, bulletin, 18–21
Bookshelf, parent, 84–85
Boredom, 52
Bulletin boards, 18–21, 84
  in special education classes, 103
Bullying Beyond the Schoolyard: Preventing and Responding to Cyberbullying, 54
Bus regulations and information, 11

Calculators, 61, 100
Calendars, monthly, 83
Calls, telephone, 84
  calling webs and, 81–82
  start-up, 81
Children's Literature Web Guide, 48

Classrooms
  arrangement of, 7–8, 15–17, 103
  bulletin boards in, 18–21
  environment and self-esteem, 20–21, 76
  expectations and schedules, 11, 12, 104
  full-inclusion mainstreaming in, 95–97
  humor in, 118, 120–121
  management of students with ADD/ADHD, 98–101
  parent involvement in, 80–85
  rules, 13–14
  seating plans, 11, 100
  special education, 102–105
  student participation in, 71–73
  suggestion boxes in, 82–83
  supplies, 8–9
Cody's Science Education Zone, 48
Coercive leadership, 72
Colleagues, teachers', 10, 114
Color-coded index cards, 93
Communications with parents
  methods for, 13, 80–85
  parent-teacher conferences and, 86–89
  of special needs students, 97, 100
Concept review, 44
Conclusions, jumping to, 118
Conferences
  parent-teacher, 86–89
  teacher evaluation, 108–111
Consistency, 53
Creative review, 38, 40–41
Critical-thinking skills, higher-order, 29–30
Curricular boards, 19–20
Curriculum
  first week, 11–12
  hidden, 74–75
  lesson plans, 12, 92–93, 109
  prioritizing, 34–36
  special needs students and, 11, 91–94

Desk arrangement, 15–17
Discipline, 50–56
    interactions with students needing, 75–76
Donations, classroom, 8

Emergency cards, student, 10
Emergency drills, 9
Emotional and social leadership, 72
Environment, study, 44, 45 (figure)
Evaluations, teacher, 107–111
Exceptions in rubrics, 68
Exercises, physical, 93, 105
Expectations and schedule, classroom,
    11, 12, 104
Extra-credit assignments, 13

Failing grades, 62
Fairness
    of questioning, 27
    student behavior and, 53
Family problems, 52
First day, preparing for the, 10–11
Flash cards, 43–44
Followers in group participation, 73
Formulas, grading, 64–65
Fulghum, Robert, 19
Full-inclusion mainstreaming, 95–97
Full moons, 53

Girlfriend/boyfriend problems, 52
Goals
    integration, 33–34
    reflected in rubrics, 67
Grading
    classroom participation, 73
    failing grades and, 62
    formulas, 64–65
    justifying decisions made in, 65, 88
    letter to numerical conversions in, 63–64, 88
    percentage systems for, 62
    red ink and, 58
    self-esteem and methods of, 57–59
    standards, 13
    stress and, 113
    systems, 60–65
    using calculators in, 61
Graphic organizers, 93
Greeters, classroom, 108
Group participation, 72–73

Handbooks, staff, 10
Hidden curriculum, 74–75
Higher-order critical-thinking skills, 29–30

Hinduja, Sameer, 54
Homework, 13, 34
Housekeeping procedures, 13
Humor, 118, 120–121

Ignoring negative behaviors, 54
Independence, student, 114
Index cards, color-coded, 93
Individualized education plans
    (IEPs), 11, 92
Information
    boards, 19
    for substitute teachers, 12, 22–24
Ink, red, 58
Integration, goals, 33–34
Intellectual leadership, 72
Intelligences, multiple (MI),
    38, 39–40 (table)
Interactions with students, 75–76
Interest, student
    creative review and, 38, 40–41
    creativity in keeping, 37–38
    multiple intelligences (MI) and,
        38, 39–40 (table)
Internet, the, 46–49

Jumping to conclusions, 118

Leadership personality traits, 71–73
Leaders in group participation, 72
Lesson plans, 12, 109
    special needs students and, 92–93
Letter grades, 63–64
Listening centers, 93
Lunch procedures, 9

Maal, Nusa, 93
Mainstreaming, full-inclusion, 95–97
Management of students with ADD/
    ADHD, 98–101
Mapping Inner Space, 93
Maps, story, 93
Margulies, Nancy, 93
Math Forum @Drexel, 48
Medication, student use of, 52–53, 99
Memorable teaching moments, 117–121
Mistakes, accepting, 114
Modeling respect, 77
Monthly calendars, 83
Moons, full, 53
Motivators, 13
Multiple intelligences (MI), 38,
    39–40 (table)

Nametags, student, 10
Negative emotions and teachers, 53
Negative student behavior, 51–54, 119
Newsletters, weekly, 84
No Child Left Behind Act, 20, 42, 66
Nonacademic activities in special education
     classes, 105
Non-English-speaking parents, 84
Nonparticipants in group participation, 73
Numerical grades, 63–64, 88

Observation, teacher, 108–109
Office hours, 83
Organized chance questioning, 28–29

Parents
     beginning of the year questionnaires
          for, 82
     bookshelf, 84–85
     calling webs and, 81–82
     communications with, 13, 80–85
     correspondence with, 12
     donations to classrooms, 8
     full-inclusion mainstreaming and
          communication with, 97
     involvement in classrooms, 80–85
     monthly calendars for, 83
     non-English speaking, 84
     office hours and, 83
     room, 84
     start-up calls to, 81
     suggestion boxes for, 82–83
     -teacher conferences, 86–89
     Thursday folder notes to, 83
     welcome letters to, 11
     who can't read, 119
Participation, student, 71–73
Patchin, Justin W., 54
Percentage systems for grading, 62
Personal family problems, 52
Philosophical boards, 19
Physical exercises, 93, 105
Placement tests, 105
Positive, accentuating the, 59
Post-observation conferences, 110–111
Power standards, 35
Preparations
     first day, 10–11
     stress and, 113
Prioritizing curricula, 34–36
Procedures
     establishing, 12–14
     school, 9–10, 12–13
Profiles, student, 76–77
Pullout sessions, 9

Questioning
     fairness of, 27
     higher-order critical-thinking skills
          and, 29–30
     organized chance, 28–29
     roll book-pattern, 28
     seating-pattern, 27
Questionnaires, beginning
     of the year, 82

Recess procedures, 9
Red ink, grading in, 58
Respect, 14
     modeling, 77
Review
     concept, 44
     creative, 38, 40–41
Rewards and incentives, 13
Roll book-pattern questioning, 28
Room parents, 84
Routines, daily, 13
Rubrics
     examples of, 69 (table)
     exceptions in, 68
     goals reflected in, 67
     No Child Left Behind standards
          and, 66–67
     specificity of, 67–68
Rules, class, 13–14

SARK, 19
School(s)
     bulletins, 12
     information, gathering, 9–10
     procedures, 9–10, 12–13
     rules for students, 10
Seating-pattern questioning, 27
Seating plans, 11, 100
Section 504 (504s), 11
Self-esteem
     classroom environment and, 20–21, 76
     discipline and, 75–76
     hidden curriculum and, 74–75
     marking papers and promoting, 57–59
     respect and, 14, 77
     student profiles and, 76–77
Show-off boards, 20–21
Slash marks in grading, 58
Social and emotional leadership, 72
Special education classes
     bulletin boards in, 103
     classroom introductions in, 103–104
     first days in, 105
     physical classroom arrangement for, 103
     tips for success in, 104–105

Special needs students
    ADD/ADHD, 52–53, 82, 98–101
    classroom management of, 98–101
    classrooms for, 102–105
    communication with parents of, 97, 100
    full inclusion mainstreaming of, 95–97
    modifying classroom curriculum
        for, 11, 91–94
    nonacademic activities for, 105
    physical exercise by, 93, 105
    placement tests for, 105
    See also Students
Specificity of rubrics, 67–68
Sponge activities, 12
Staff
    handbooks, 10
    support, 10, 96–97
Standardized testing, 42–43
Standards, power, 35
Start-up calls, 81
Story maps, 93
Stress, 112–115
Students
    calculators used by, 100
    creative review for, 38, 40–41
    desk arrangements, 15–17
    donations to the classroom, 8–9
    full-inclusion mainstreaming of, 95–97
    independence, 114
    interactions with, 75–76
    medication use by, 52–53, 99
    multiple intelligences (MI) and,
        38, 39–40 (table)
    nametags, 10
    negative behavior by, 51–54, 119
    participation in classrooms, 71–73
    physical exercise by, 93, 105
    present at parent-teacher conferences, 87
    profiles, 76–77
    seating plans, 11, 100
    self-esteem, 20–21
    signals for gaining attention from, 11, 99
    See also Special needs students
Study
    environment, 44, 45 (figure)
    flash cards for, 43–44
    reviewing concepts in, 44
Subject areas
    integrating goals and, 33–34
    using multiple intelligences (MI) in teaching,
        38, 39–40 (table)
    Web sites, 48–49

Substitute teachers, 12, 22–24
Suggestion boxes, 82–83
Support staff, 10, 96–97

Task leadership, 72
Taxonomy, Bloom's, 29–30
Teachers
    being human, 54
    colleagues, 10, 114
    conferences with parents,
        86–89
    in control of classrooms, 51
    evaluations, 107–111
    excitement and frustration of, 1–2
    ignoring negative behavior, 54
    individual styles, 54
    interactions with students,
        75–76
    Internet resources for, 46–49
    jumping to conclusions, 118
    lesson plans, 12, 92–93, 109
    memorable teaching moments,
        117–121
    modeling respect, 77
    office hours, 83
    procedures established by, 13–14
    showing negative emotion, 53
    stress, 112–115
    substitute, 12, 22–24
    team-teaching by, 117
Teachers Helping Teachers, 47
Team-teaching, 117
Telephone calls. See Calls, telephone
Temporary support assistant
    (TSA), 96–97
Test-taking skills, 42–45
Thursday folder notes, 83, 84
Time management
    homework and, 34
    integrating goals for, 33–34
    making choices and, 34–36
Translations, 84

URLs. See Internet, the

Webs, calling, 81–82
Web sites. See Internet, the
Weekly newsletters, 84
Welcome letters to parents, 11
World Wide Art Resource, 49

X marks in grading, 58

CORWIN

A SAGE Company

The Corwin logo—a raven striding across an open book—represents the union of courage and learning. Corwin is committed to improving education for all learners by publishing books and other professional development resources for those serving the field of PreK–12 education. By providing practical, hands-on materials, Corwin continues to carry out the promise of its motto: **"Helping Educators Do Their Work Better."**